Scribe Pu
MODERN I

Neil James

Neil James was born in Cooma and educated in Sydney,
a doctorate in English while working as an editor and a book reviewer. In 2003, Neil established the Plain English Foundation with Dr Peta Spear to improve the quality of Australian public language. The foundation has since trained some 10,000 professional people. Neil chairs the International Plain Language Working Group and features regularly in the media throughout Australia. The latest of his three books is *Writing at Work*, and he has published more than 60 articles, reviews, and essays on language and literature.

Harold Scruby

Harold 'Haitch' Scruby was born in Singapore and educated in Sydney. During his 25 years in the rag trade, he wrote two books: *Waynespeak* and *Manglish*. He spent eight years on Mosman Council as a councillor and deputy mayor. In 1996, he became chairman of the not-for-profit Pedestrian Council of Australia. Harold is a passionate crusader for pedestrians, particularly 'walking families – moving forward', and the executive director of Ausflag Limited, which wants the jack removed from the Australian flag. He has written articles for Australia's leading newspapers, and his favourite quip is one of Jerry Seinfeld's: 'I love the Australian flag ... Britain at night.'

Alan Moir

Alan Moir was born and educated in New Zealand, and moved to Australia in the early 1970s. He has been an editorial cartoonist for *The Bulletin* and *The Courier-Mail*, and is now an editorial cartoonist for *The Sydney Morning Herald*. Alan has published several books, and his work is held in collections in Australia and overseas. He has won the Stanley Award for Editorial Cartoonist of the Year six times, as well as the Walkley Award for Excellence in Journalism in 2000 and 2006. He was runner-up in the United Nations Correspondents Association Ranan Lurie Political Cartoon Award in 2004.

MODERN MANGLISH

Gobbledygook Made Plain

Neil James & Harold Scruby
Illustrations by Alan Moir

SCRIBE
Melbourne

Scribe Publications Pty Ltd
18–20 Edward St, Brunswick, Victoria, Australia 3056
Email: info@scribepub.com.au

First published by Scribe 2011

Typeset in 10.5/14pt Legacy Serif ITC by the publishers
Printed and bound in Australia by Griffin Press
Only wood grown from sustainable regrowth forests is used in the manufacture of paper found in this book.

National Library of Australia
Cataloguing-in-Publication data

James, Neil, 1966–
Scruby, Harold, 1947–

Modern Manglish: gobbledygook made plain.

9781921844508 (pbk.)

English language—Australia—Humour.

Other Authors/Contributors:
Moir, Alan, 1947–

427.994

Plain English Foundation

www.scribepublications.com.au

CONTENTS

FOREWORD

Caroline Jones AO

When Prime Minister Gillard accused Tony Abbott of high dungeon over the carbon tax, she graduated from enthusiastic amateur to consummate Manglish professional. Her daybyou with hyperbowl had shown promise, but this left it for dead in one fowl swoop. I checked Hansard to see if the record had been corrected for the sake of proprietary. Fortunately not, so the PM's achievement stands, for posterity, as the remarkable phenomena that it is.

My next thought was, never mind a carbon tax – why not a tax on Manglish because, at this point in time, we're all at it, 24/7. A mangle tax would net the government a bonanza, returning the budget to surplus in six months. Just for a start, the pandemic of feral apostrophes would bring in miwyons, and our exuberant circumcision of syntax would soon cancel the national debt.

But I transgress. Going forward, I must disclose a festered interest. While many others, as seen on ABC TV's *The Collectors*, hoard eggcups, model trains, and exotic breeds of chooks, for me the compulsion is Manglish. I can't resist collecting it.

It would be alright if my addiction were fed by Irritable Pedantry Syndrome (IPS) – appropriate to a senior citizen. But yeah-no, I fall upon each new morsel of modern Manglish with gleeful delight. I relish it. It makes me laugh out loud, especially when it falls from the lips of our leaders.

One of our science supremos says that he is concerned about climate-change denialists. That may seem a poultry slip to you. It's food and drink to me. As Dame Edna said, so memorably, she's been gifted by Mother Nature with the capacity to laugh at the misfortune of others. I wonder if I may be similarly afflicted?

It's a sobering thought, especially since her proud announcement that, in memory of her late husband, Norm, she is now patron of the Prostrate Olympics, which will feature a plethaura of aquatic events, in keeping with the nature of the illness.

For all its moments of triumphant acquisition, at the end of the day gathering mangles can be a lonely pastime. Imagine, then, my glad relief at the publication of this iconic volume of modern Manglish. Should you also be a devotee of the jonrah, I commend it to you as welcome reassurance that we are not alone in our obsession. I believe that this splendid book initiates a new narrative in the Strayan vernacular.

INTRODUCTION

Let's begin with an admission: our mongrel tongue is so rich and complex that all of us, at times, mangle our English. But if we might borrow from George Orwell's *Animal Farm*: all of us mangle, but some mangle more than others.

The national broadcaster can now lead with the breathless story that our team's World Cup campaign 'hangs by a thread' after 'a stoic draw' in which they 'could've thrown in the towel', but 'dug deep to almost snatch a win'. Then a commentator can offer the incisive analysis that a swimmer 'swum a better time than what he swum in the Olympics'.

These are just two of the pillars of poor public language: unthinking cliché and the mishandling of tenses. A Manglish double twist with pike.

Does this matter? In the information age, should we worry over every ephemeral expression? Should our task be to capture language as it changes, rather than prescribe a linguistic cod-liver oil?

We think that quality public language does matter. It matters when we make our communication so ordinary that it is pitched at what Randolph Stow called 'arrogant mediocrity' rather than excellence. It matters when we mix our metaphors by barking up a dry tree to seek a fair shake of the sauce bottle while sticking our neck out on a limb. It matters when we discover the true fact that each of us individually can reiterate again very unique tautologies that fail to prevent Manglish recurring in the future.

Forgetting that this matters meant that we tossed grammar out of our school system, depriving our children of the tools they need to understand what a sentence is – let alone what makes one effective. As a result, we have dumbed down two generations to the point where even intelligent youngsters possess the communication skills of dullards. Teenage conversation is now full of phatic phrases such as 'Yeah-no. She went, like, you know and that, but, and I went, um, like, you know, right!' So why are we surprised when we hear that 'Me and Wayne went to the footy'? Or that they don't know the difference between 'your' and 'you're'? Or that we better had a whole nother pacific reason for making that insinuendo.

Growing up online in an American world may be part of the problem. Apple's iSlogan urges us to 'think different'. And why learn about tenses when Honey 'shrunk the kids'? When American idiom has us 'laying down', like hens, before we 'come by' your house because we 'can't hardly wait' for the next double negative? When we verb respectable nouns without blinking? And when the adverb has virtually disappeared from the language?

It also matters in the workplace when we write in a style that is inefficient and hard to fathom. In the absence of an ability to conversate at this point in time, we are of the considered opinion that there is a negative good in taking on board the narrative on the basis of the fact that we can't remember what we meant to say at the start of this sentence. So we drop into suitspeak to cover off on all bases and incentivise our stakeholders while we drill down to upticking the boxes and work towards singing from the same hymn sheet. Going forwards. Saying nothing.

This is where we find the worst manglers, and this is where it really matters. Suits and politicians deliberately latch on to jargon to paper over the unpleasant, and to diminish our capacity to call them to account. They 'relanguage' a deadline until it becomes an 'aspirational time horizon', and turn a new tax into 'an investment in human capital'. At the end of the day, they take 'strategic staircases' to avoid 'detailed programmatic specificity' in relation to 'legacy assets'.

All of this matters. But it doesn't mean that all change is suspect. English-speakers around the world are creating hundreds of new words a year, many of which are acceptable, colourful, and meaningful. But if we acquiesce to change, we abrogate our responsibility to democracy. As citizens, we will be as effective as the illiterate protest signs warning that we are 'loosing our constitutional rights' to those interventionist 'pubic servants'.

We wrote *Modern Manglish* because we believe that English matters. We also believe that the best way to battle the worst excesses of our public language is to laugh at them. But while you enjoy the malaprops and mixed metaphors, the buzzwords and doublespeak, and the pollie waffle and clichés, think about where Manglish is intruding into your everyday encounters. Then share your experience at www.manglish.com.au so we can laugh at it together. To understand Manglish at its best, we must, above all else, keep our sense o' yuma.

DOUBLESPEAK AND VERBING

Unremarkably, languages grow or die. To keep them relevant and effective, we are constantly coining new terms for new concepts, changing the meanings of words, and altering the way in which others function. Think for a moment about the evolving application of the word 'gay':

> **Boys and girls come out to play, happy and gay the Laxette way.**
>
> **Laugh, Kookaburra; laugh, Kookaburra; gay your life must be.**

The children and the kookaburra in these ditties were initially simple, joyous, and cheerful beings, until the shifting meaning of 'gay' gave them a sexual preference. And now we are even turning them into something uncool. When a certain politician tried to lecture his daughter about drugs, she told him not to be such a 'lame, gay, churchy loser'.

At times, these changes in meaning introduce negative connotations. Being 'sinister' used to mean simply left-handed, while 'sly' originally meant clever. 'Awful' once only inspired awe rather than being terrible, something 'artificial' had true artistic value, and even a 'pirate' was originally a small (not necessarily in stature) businessman. The process can also happen in reverse: something 'terrific' used to cause genuine terror, a 'brave' person was actually uncivilised, and being 'nice' meant that you were ignorant.

The great democratic glory of English is that the broader community ends up deciding if particular words will change their meaning. But if we want that democracy to function well, it shouldn't mean that anything goes.

There is a line not to cross. Stepping over that line leads to Manglish.

Doublespeak

Manglish begins when we deliberately set out to give words new meanings in order to make them fancier, soften a harsher reality, or paper over something unpleasant. This is the Manglish of doublespeak. Here are some examples:

Aspirational time horizon
Deadline

Career transition program
Sacking

Civilian irregular defence staff
Mercenaries

Collateral damage
Dead civilians

Delivery commitment
Guarantee

Deployment of forces
Invasion

Disintermediate
Cut out the middle man

Flexibilise
Deregulate

Gratuity payment
Bribe

Handyman's dream
Run-down house

Investment in human capital
Tax

Job flexibility
Casual employment

Legacy asset
Toxic debt

Liquidity backstop
Government bailout

Preventative detention
Imprisonment without trial

Public diplomacy
Propaganda

Relanguage
Rewrite

Removal pathway
Deportation

Strategic staircase
Plan

The rich seam of doublespeak runs so abundantly through the strata of Manglish – from euphemisms and suitspeak to mission statements and fancy-pants job titles – that we'll be mining it further in several dedicated chapters.

Verbing

While we remain on guard against the latest doublespeak, there is another process to watch out for: verbing. This coinage takes a perfectly good noun and turns it, unnecessarily, into a verb.

Sports commentators and journalists are very good at this process, probably because they desperately try to think of new ways to describe what are essentially the same actions. An Australian newspaper recently decided to accept 'medal' as a verb:

> Anton Ohno can become the most medalled American Winter Olympian in the 1000m.

Perhaps it was following the lead of the UK Olympic team:

> The team includes athletes who have medalled at Olympic, World, and European level, so this is an exciting proposition for the Games.

But it took swimming and skiing commentators to come up with these:

> She hasn't won an event this season, but has podiumed a couple of times.

> Her form has been so good, I'm sure that she'll podium tonight. Remember that she silvered in Athens.

Of course, some of these new verbal coinages catch on. For instance, 'texting' has become useful to describe sending an

instant message by mobile phone. In this case, 'text' already had some history as a verb. In the 16th century, it meant 'to cite text' or 'to write text in-hand'. Those uses became rare or obsolete, so 'text' humbly reverted to a noun. Now 'texting' with a mobile phone simply resurrects the verb form in a new context.

'Medalling' may already be a lost cause, but it's hard to see 'podiuming' taking on. And there are others that we should resist:

To antique ('We went antiquing on the weekend.')

To auralise ('He couldn't auralise the instruments.')

To best ('I bested him at squash.')

To boomerang ('The plan boomeranged on us.')

To bottom-line ('He did not bottom-line the budget.')

To ceiling ('The prices ceilinged around June.')

To contemporise ('Let's contemporise these events.')

To contracept ('He had no idea of contracepting.')

To diagram ('Can you diagram that idea for me?')

To diarise ('I forgot to diarise the appointment!')

To dollarise ('If I could dollarise the project …')

To expense ('We can expense this lunch.')

To gift ('Gran gifted me more socks.')

To green-light ('Let's green-light this proposal.')

To grow ('We are growing the business.')

To guest ('I'm guesting on that program again.')

To harsh ('Stop harshing all my ideas.')

To incentivate ('We'll incentivate our employees.')

To incentivise ('Cash bonuses incentivise workers.')

To keyboard ('Can you keyboard this for me?')

To offline ('We should offline this discussion.')

To schematise ('Scientists schematised the various experiments.')

To springboard ('That springboarded my career.')

To strategise ('Let's strategise our solution to this problem.')

To synergise ('We'll synergise our processes.')

To tenant ('We've tenanted the place for six months.')

To value-add ('The new version doesn't value-add existing products.')

To verbal ('Police verballed him.')

To verbalise ('Make sure you verbalise your issues.')

To verse ('Who are you versing this weekend?')

To vocalise ('I want you to vocalise your concerns.')

To waste ('He was accused of wasting a gang member.')

TAUTOLOGIES AND OTHER REDUNDANCIES

Tautologies are the greatest breeding ground for Manglish. It is here that politicians and priests, sports commentators and corporate leaders, all sink proudly into the mire, blissfully unaware of their excesses. Indeed, so great is their hubris that they are not averse to repeating their errors in the belief that repetition can only reinforce their words.

Probably the best example is those who leave their phones permanently on voicemail with the message: 'I'm currently unavailable at the moment. I'm either on the phone, away from my desk, or busy defying gravity.' Who cares? And why do they compound a tautology with such superfluous nonsense? We know that they are unavailable because they didn't answer.

A tautology, needless to say, is the repetition of an idea or a statement using other words. For example:

> He did a lot of running with his legs today.

Not that it got him very far:

> He's missed two caught and bowled opportunities — both off his own bowling.

And who was he, anyway?

If I keep getting Boyd and O'Grady mixed up it's because they look so alike, particularly around the head.

And here is a mind-boggling fact from another sports commentator:

The stadium is close to capacity — as far as full is concerned.

But there is nothing like a positive outlook, and here sports commentators seem to excel:

A boxer makes a comeback for one of two reasons: either he's broke or he needs the money.

Here he is. Yesterday's winner. The man who won yesterday.

If we were talking positively, I can't see no reason why Christie can't get a medal.

I'm going to make a prediction — it could go either way.

I really expect it to go one way or the other tonight.

Of course, one of [snooker player] Stephen Hendry's greatest assets is his ability to score when he's playing.

Or simply:

It was a goal of really simple simplicity.

And seen from the competitor's view:

I hope to come first or second, or at least win it.

Then there was the sprinter who told us:

My personal best time was better than my best.

And one final word from our competitors:

We're very pleased about the way we played because we know we can play like that.

Right. The Manglish of sport is so highly developed that we'll be giving it a whole chapter later on. For now, we can get away from sport to some examples we found from other fields, such as this:

> London isn't the largest city, but it's definitely larger than the next largest.

And what is the best way to appreciate this vast metropolis?

> You only have to fly over it or go in a helicopter.

We heard an earnest young graduate say in a meeting:

> We need to prevent this happening again at some point of time in the future.

And from a Sydney meteorologist:

> It's been raining for eight consecutive days in a row.

One famous political leader announced after an election:

> We didn't win, but we didn't lose.

And another well-known politician who had an unenviable reputation for tautologies came up with the following:

> It's all summed up in the crux of one situation.

> Queensland is not prepared to put its feet on the sticking paper and be stuck with it.

> We stick like glue and we work like glue.

> We won't be able to sit on uranium. Firstly because it would not be right, and secondly because it would be wrong.

Other utterances of the great man included:

> We have to get the status quo back to what it was before.

The secret of my success is that I don't beat around the bush and say exactly what I mean.

But perhaps one of the most frequent and unconscious tautologies of all is the phrase 'I'm going to go.'

There are many other tautologies, admittedly less spectacular, which have found a permanent home in our language. The following are just some of the tautologies that are daily occurrences. Believe us.

ABN number

Actual thing itself

Added bonus

And, etc.

Annual AGM

Around about

As near as near

ATM machine

Back back straight into another car

The bargain basement downstairs

Circle around the block

Collaborate together

Come back again

The current climate at the moment

Debate about

Different varieties

Each of you individually

An essential prerequisite

Exactly the same thing

The extra thing I have added is

Family heirloom

FBT tax

Filthy dirty pig

Final upshot

Finally finished

Forward progress

Free gifts

Further additions

Future prospects

Grateful thanks

Greetings and salutations

Human-made synthetic

I have experienced this before

I'll just clean up the mess

In a row one after another

Internationally around the world

It gave me some bad adverse effects

It's re-echoed

It was cut into two halves

I used to do that before

Join together in unison

Kills flies and cockies dead

Last will and testament

Letter in writing

Lob the ball high up into the air

Male bachelor

Male penis

Meaningless mission statement

Mix together

My ancestors were original First Fleeters

My own car

Nationally around the country

Never once

New novelty

Null and void

Old, outdated material

One and the same

The other alternative

Overseas imports

Past experience

Past history

PIN number

Pregnant with child

A preliminary preamble

Pre-plan

Pre-prepare

Preset

Raging out of control

Reason why

Recall back

Reduce down

Reiterate again

Repay back

Repeat again

Restate again

REVERSING BACKWARDS

Returning for a comeback

Reverse backwards

Right now

Round about

Rural and regional

SMS message

So incredible I could scarcely believe it

Stupid idiot

Sufficient enough

The sum total

Tediously boring

There's no need for undue worry

Toxic poisons

A true fact

Two twins

Unique, never-to-be-repeated offer

Vacuous vision statement

Very true

Watch the vision

When I first founded the company

Wholly new innovation

4.00 a.m. in the morning

6.00 p.m. in the evening

CLICK GO THE CLICHÉS

A cliché is an expression so worn out that it offers almost no meaning. It is a regular favourite of all Manglish speakers because it saves time and effort. While there is probably nothing wrong with an occasional cliché, overuse means that we end up letting our clichés do our thinking for us. As George Orwell observed, we assemble a sentence much like a prefabricated henhouse.

Politicians are particularly adept at verbal henhouses. They learn early that clichés give the appearance of saying something without committing to anything:

> I believe that the government had lost its way, and I intend to have a conversation with the Australian people so that we can canvass the best ways to move forward and all work together in the national interest.

This all sounds positive enough. But what will it actually deliver?

Perhaps the worst crime of the cliché is that it is oh-so-predictable and oh-so-boring. Admittedly, it is hard to come up with fresh phrases and images every day. So the cliché waits eagerly for its opportunity to leap onto the page.

Cliché One: the overworked phrase

The first category of cliché is the easiest to turn to when you must say something but have nothing to offer. Just add conjunctions.

All things being equal

Best thing since sliced bread

Better late than never

Boys will be boys

Burn the midnight oil

Conspicuous by one's absence

Dose of your own medicine

Easier said than done

Going around in circles

Heart of gold

I'd give my right arm

Just like Mother used to make

Keep your shirt on

Last but not least

Lay down the law

Let's get the show on the road

Life wasn't meant to be easy

Moment you've been waiting for

More than meets the eye

No rest for the wicked

Off the beaten track

Out of sight, out of mind

Point of no return

Powers that be

Put your money where your mouth is

Road to perdition

Second to none

See light at the end of the tunnel

Short and sweet

Shoulder to cry on

Show must go on

Sight for sore eyes

Slave over a hot stove

Through thick and thin

To cut a long story short

Too good to be true

Two's company, three's a crowd

Water under the bridge

With all due respect

You can't win 'em all

You took the words right out of my mouth

Cliché Two: the threadbare quotation

While overused phrases can 'slip under your radar', the threadbare quotation is easier to detect. Users of these clichés are often convinced that they are displaying great erudition by quoting from fable and folklore, from biblical and literary genius.

All's fair in love and war

All things must pass

An apple a day keeps the doctor away

Beauty is in the eye of the beholder

A bird in the hand is worth two in the bush

Blood is thicker than water

Blood, sweat, and tears

Cast pearls before swine

Don't count your chickens before they hatch

The early bird catches the worm

A fool and his money are soon parted

A friend in need is a friend indeed

The fruits of one's labours

Hell hath no fury like a woman scorned

Hope springs eternal

Labour of love

Land of milk and honey

Lend me your ears

Like two ships passing in the night

Milk of human kindness

More sinned against than sinning

Necessity is the mother of invention

Neither a borrower nor a lender be

No man is an island

Not with a bang but a whimper

A picture paints a thousand words

A pound of flesh

The slings and arrows of outrageous fortune

Still waters run deep

Survival of the fittest

There, but for the grace of God, go I

Time heals all wounds

To thine own self be true

Truth is stranger than fiction

The tyranny of distance

When in Rome, do as the Romans do

Without further ado

Worth one's weight in gold

Cliché Three: the frayed figure of speech

Our final category of cliché compares something with an example, mostly via the verb 'to be' or a linking word such as 'like' or 'as'. Whenever someone coins a fresh simile or metaphor, we all leap on it until it gets old and stale. The worst examples hang around like a bad smell, much as limpets cling to a rock:

It's a dog's life

It's a small world

Lap of luxury

Life and soul of the party

Life is just a bowl of cherries

Life's a bitch, and then you die

Like a bat out of hell

Load off my mind

Make a mountain out of a molehill

More than one way to skin a cat

My heart bleeds for you

The name of the game

Once in a blue moon

Par for the course

Pillar of society

Plenty more fish in the sea

Quick as a wink

Seize the bull by the horns

A shot in the dark

Skating on thin ice

The sky is the limit

Snake in the grass

Snug as a bug in a rug

Strike while the iron is hot

Thick as thieves

The tip of the iceberg

Tower of strength

Turning in her/his grave

Ugly as sin

Until hell freezes over

Until the cows come home

Warm the cockles of your heart

A whole new ball game

Work one's fingers to the bone

String examples from all three categories together, and we have the perfect pre-fabricated henhouse of a paragraph:

> Be that as it may, when we arrived bright-eyed and bushy-tailed it was not to batten down the hatches. Just as night follows day, it goes without saying that we have opened a Pandora's box. While we won't beat a hasty retreat, you can bet your bottom dollar we'll go back to the drawing board to come up with a brand spanking new idea that will allow us to pass with flying colours and depart in a blaze of glory.

BUZZWORDS

In ancient times, we were taught that less was more, simplicity meant clarity, and short words were easier to understand than long ones. Mark Twain famously implored us not to 'use a five-dollar word when a fifty-cent word will do'. We would like to think that this still holds true, but some livelihoods apparently depend on the ability to complicate language. They start with buzzwords to make their content sound busier than it is.

At this point in time
Now

Come onstream
Start

Conversate
Talk

Down the track
Later

Due to the fact that
Because

Evidenced in a written manner
In writing

Facilitate the identification of
Help to find

Genre
Category

Has an obligation to
Must

Has the capability to
Can

In accordance with your request
As you asked

In a timely manner
Promptly

In the absence of
Without

In the near future

Soon

In this day and age

Now

Is of the considered opinion that

Thinks

It will be necessary to advise this office

You must let us know

It would be appreciated if you would ascertain whether

Please find out if

Narrative

Story

Negative good

Bad

On the basis of the fact that

Because

The question was completed in the negative

No

Take on board

Agree

Together with the associated

With

Up and running

Operating

Will endeavour to provide you with

Will try to send you

The most common buzzword-manglers are government departments (abetted by lawyers), which like to string complex phrases together until they sound like this:

> In accordance with your request, and in consideration of the fact that significant time has elapsed, it is incumbent upon you to facilitate the identification of the certificate. It would be appreciated if you would ascertain this information in a timely manner.

Ironically, the level of government closest to the people is often the worst, as this letter from a local council attests:

> In terms of reaching its decision, Council took into consideration the matters in your submission and, as the proposal complied with the objectives of Council's policies and conformed to the relevant statutory requirements, Council was of the opinion that the application should be approved.

But it takes a top-notch government report to reach the apotheosis of policyspeak:

> Government failure is a technical term that, rather than implying that governments have failed, recognises that government objectives and information can change over time. Government failure is also referred to as government policy in chapter one of this report.

Lest the private sector start feeling too smug, we should point out that every profession is prone to its very own set of buzzwords. An editor was once working on an engineering report that explained a construction project to the public. One passage detailed how a pipeline would be sprayed with cement until it 'attains negative buoyancy'.

'You mean "until it sinks"?' the editor asked.

'No,' the engineer argued, 'it must read "attain negative buoyancy".'

'So it won't sink?'

'Well, yes.'

'So may we write "sink"?'

'No, because it *attains negative buoyancy*.'

Buzzwords.

The staff in another organisation asked their finance department for help in completing a financial return. What was a 'contingent liability', they queried? Easy, wrote finance:

> Contingent liabilities are possible liabilities that arise from past events, the existence of which will be confirmed only by the occurrence or non-occurrence of one or more uncertain future events not wholly within the control of the entity.

But for truly impressive buzzwords, it is useful to turn to the world of medicine, which does an excellent job at dressing

up simple ideas in Latin and Greek. Here's a sample from a medical journal:

> Initially, gagging and tongue-pulling manoeuvres were attempted with no change in symptomatology. Digital rectal massage was then attempted using a slow, circumferential motion. The frequency of hiccups immediately began to slow, with a termination of all hiccups within 30 seconds.

Once we'd translated that advice, we decided that the cure was worse than the disease.

Then there is artspeak, which requires a whole new set of abstractions to describe what are usually concrete things. Here's one about a painter:

> It's as if the catastrophic undoing that functions like an aesthetic principle in Millar's art begins to look like the refracted image of a catastrophic contemporaneity.

And another, describing dance:

> Aspirations to overcome the constraints of time, place, and physical capacity are mediated by memories and technologies. But the gap between individual aspirations and the uniformity of ensemble behaviour is not so thoroughly explored. Individual imperatives to 'take me there' are met with collective actions in response that set limits and refusals.

Don't ask. We have no idea what that means, either.

The first prize for over-complexity must go to the academy, where each discipline generates its own set of buzzwords, regardless of how simple the ideas actually are. The following comes from a book about cultural exchange between Asia and Australia. All it means is that when you migrate to a new country, you'll always feel outside the culture of that country. But that won't get anyone tenure like this passage:

> Whether you discuss this open/closed in terms of the semiotic coding of the self and other, some kind of introjected and extrojected cultural imago, or the cross-projection of Lacanian veils on a cultural plane — each of which generates different kinds of problematics and solutions — it nevertheless remains a cross-cultural rule of thumb that 'out' is not 'in' because 'in' is the inverse of 'out'.

Then there is this example (from the communications department of a university!):

> Although the culturally sedimented practices precluding the possibility of a different interfield dynamic are considerable, I conclude by 'visualising' an alternative relationship, one constituted, on all sides, by what Williams Connolly (2005) characterises as a properly democratic ethos of 'agonistic respect' across difference.

So do buzzwords work? The evidence suggests not. In a study called 'Consequences of Erudite Vernacular Utilized Irrespective of Necessity', Daniel M. Oppenheimer found that 90 per cent of undergraduates admitted to using complicated language to sound more intelligent, and nearly 70 per cent used a thesaurus to choose more-complicated words. But he found that these students generally scored worse than those using simple language.

As Winston Churchill once said: 'Short words are best, and the old words when short are best of all.'

SUITSPEAK

Suitspeak is corporate jargon. To be kind, it's bullshit: a language spoken by the big end of town to hypnotise and confuse employees, investors, and customers alike. Its speakers are a bit like the upper-class English, who pronounce words in certain ways to define themselves as part of an elite.

Too often, suitspeak clichés seem to be as fashionable as the teenage use of 'like'. 'Going forwards' is a classic example. Compulsory in almost every sentence, it's the new 'um', 'er', or 'der' – only with a dollar attached. Over time, suitspeak trickles down to middle managers, who mimic the clichés of their superiors like ventriloquists' dummies, as in the following examples:

Attain world's best practice
Reach the highest standard

Benchmark
Measure

Blue-sky thinking
Original/creative thinking

Bricks and mortar
Buildings

Core competencies
Strengths or requirements

Cover all the bases
Check everything

Cover off on that
Check/finalise/fix that

Drill down
Look at the detail

Drink the Kool-Aid
Take the company line

Eat your own dog food
Use your own products

Give a heads-up
Explain or warn of a problem

Grow a business
Develop a business

Improve our synergy
Work together well

Incentivise/ Incentivation
Motivate/motivation

It's not rocket science
It's not difficult

Key stakeholders
Those most affected by an organisation

BLUE SKY THINKING

Level playing field
Fair environment

Marketing collateral
Marketing material

On-sell/up-sell/down-sell
Sell

Outcomes
Results

Paradigm shift
Major change

Pathways
Directions

Pick the low-hanging fruit
Solve the easy problems

Proactive
Active

Put all our ducks in a row
Get everything in order

Quantum leap
Major change

Robust
Strong or frank

Run it up the flagpole and see how it flies
Get feedback from others

Sing from the same hymn sheet
Take the same position

Take it offline
Talk privately

Think outside the box/square/circle
Think creatively

Tick the right boxes
Work well

And here are some of the latest corporate clichés, coming soon to a workplace near you:

Bizmeth
Business method

Boil the ocean
Take on an overwhelming problem

Circling the drain
About to go broke

Communicate telephonically
Talk on the phone

Connect the silos
Talk to each other

Engage in ideation
Think of a new idea

Harsh my mellow
Spoil a good mood

Leverage our knowledge capital
Have a new idea

Nano-manager
Incredibly picky manager

Open the kimono
Be transparent

Post a negative profit
Report a loss

Reinvent the flat tyre
Make the same mistake twice

Solutionary
A worker who develops 'revolutionary solutions'

Two-comma project
Anything costing more than $1 million

Uptick
Tick

But wait, there's more – clichés are just the beginning. The next step is to add some technical jargon. After all, why talk about improving customer service when you can:

> Consider what functionality this single end-to-end business solution provides out of the box in order to meet the functionalities these scenarios demand.

Or explain your strategy in this way:

> I'm not envisaging us doing dramatic step-outs domestically but rather bulking up the positions we've got organically.

Above all, the strategy of suitspeak is that if it sounds impressive, people will buy it even if they don't understand it. Just like this service, right?

> As a means of simultaneously decomposing both the optative and indicative parts of a requirements problem from an abstract business level to concrete system requirements, we

leverage the paradigm of projection in both approaches while maintaining traceability to high-level business objectives.

Rumour has it that, not long ago, an Australian prime minister decided to update our national anthem. Naturally, he turned to some suits for help. Here's the result:

National stakeholders going forwards should be committed to visionary communications
Australians all let us rejoice

For we incubate next-generation scenarios that leverage dynamic functionalities
For we are young and free

With mission-critical infrastructure to maximise world-class deliverables
With golden soil and wealth for toil

Our brickware harnesses frictionless supply-chain scenarios
Our home is girt by sea

Unfortunately, the text suffered from 'a high-end negative architecture scenario', which means the words wouldn't actually fit the music. The idea was scrapped.

Suitspeak Jargon Generator

The next time you find yourself in a meeting and don't understand a word anyone is saying, simply toss in your own suitspeak. Fortunately, this is easy to generate at random:

1. Take some verbs, especially those that are really nouns.
2. Add some adjectives that sound impressive without saying anything.
3. Round it off with the most impressive abstract nouns that you can muster.
4. Mix them up at random, and you are ready to bamboozle.

Optimise next-generation scenarios.

Facilitate some high-end methodologies.

Incubate visionary architectures.

Leverage holistic functionalities.

No-one will understand you, but they'll think you are leveraging an enterprising architecture of blue-sky thinking that will generate cutting-edge deliverables.

On the following page there is a table of randomised words to get you started.

Verb	Adjective	Noun
strategise	frictionless	scenarios
generate	seamless	infrastructure
facilitate	granular	content
optimise	integrated	action points
incentivate	scalable	models
innovate	transparent	solutions
streamline	mission-critical	schemes
leverage	impactful	users
synthesise	next-generation	communities
utilise	cutting-edge	deliverables
harness	visionary	architectures
integrate	high-end	supply chains
incubate	holistic	markets
engage	24/7	stakeholders
implement	strategic	methodologies
empower	dynamic	relationships
deliver	efficient	brickware
enable	customer-centric	technologies
engineer	enterprising	functionalities
transform	world-class	convergence

Suitspin

Of course, suitspeak really comes into its own when things go wrong and the suits need to avoid all responsibility. That's when it's time for a heartfelt session of blamestorming and a healthy dose of suitspin. An airline, for example, that has a slight problem with a plane crash-landing can simply describe it as:

> A sudden and unauthorised descent to an altitude below that of the runway.

The global financial crisis brought us a new golden age of suitspin. It all began with the offering of mortgages to people who could never afford them, but were talked into it with low introductory interest-rates. Here's how helpful the banks were in explaining how those rates would skyrocket after a few years:

> Before each Payment Change Date, the Note Holder will calculate the amount of the monthly payment that would be sufficient to repay the unpaid principal that I am expected to owe at the Payment Change Date in full on the Maturity Date in substantially equal instalments at the interest rate effective during the month preceding the Payment Change Date. The result of this calculation is called the 'Full Payment'.

Not wanting to hold failing mortgages themselves, financial institutions then packaged them into securities. Their carefully selected wording persuaded pension funds around the world to part with billions for complex yet worthless financial products:

Asset-backed security
Sub-prime mortgage bond

Rich security
Overpriced bond

Structured finance CDO
High-risk debt

Tranches
The floors or levels in a bond

The mezzanine
The riskiest level

And when the inevitable collapse caused company profits to plummet, those scrambling to stay alive explained it this way:

> What we're doing is, as a company, our debts have climbed over the last few years ... and we've made a decision — a company decision — to recapitalise the balance sheet. And the decision we've taken is to market the property to achieve that.

When this failed, they could simply announce a bankruptcy in the way that General Motors did to its 'key stakeholders':

> As you may know, GM is using an expedited, court-supervised process to accelerate the reinvention of our company.

Governments around the world then had to step in to save the day. Officials patiently explained the need for massive bailouts:

> If you've got a squirt gun in your pocket, you may have to take it out. If you've got a bazooka, and people know you've got it, you may not have to take it out ... By increasing confidence, it will greatly reduce the likelihood it will ever be used.

And finally, at the inevitable inquiries that followed, bank CEOs seamlessly spun how they were able to rack up such enormous losses without being aware of the risks:

> As long as the music is playing, you've got to get up and dance.

> We went through a period when once-in-10,000-year events were happening every day.

Suitspin of the century. Or the ten-by-ten century.

MIXED METAPHORS

A metaphor uses an image to capture an idea. It is one of the most useful and colourful aspects of language. If we described everything in literal terms, life would be rather boring. For example, we might say, prosaically, that someone is 'wasting time looking at something in error'. But that sounds far too abstract. How much better to say that they are 'barking up the wrong tree'?

We are constantly searching for images to convey abstract concepts because images can communicate complex ideas so simply. The problem arises when we don't think carefully enough, and select two or more images that clash. Instead of conveying a clear idea, we transmit a muddle. There's a fair chance we weren't thinking clearly at all with these:

By that stage, the death knell had been signed

Fair shake of the sauce bottle

He's as deaf as a doornail

He's buttered his bread and now he has to lie in it

He's trying to bolster up the scaffolding of a collapsing hypothesis with a red herring

I can read you like the back of my book

I can't answer that off the cuff of my head

I'm sticking my neck out on a limb

That's a case of robbing Peter to pay the piper

The leadership has gone over the top and taken fully entrenched positions

There will be a bottomless pit that will forever hang over her head

There's a heart of steel burning inside him

They're hanging on to their hats for grim life

They've got old shoulders on their heads

We'll burn that bridge when we come to it

We've got to sit down and have a think about where we stand

You can lead a horse to the river, but you can't make him water

You're barking up a dry tree

You're not the one with your arse in a noose

We are all prone to mixing metaphors in day-to-day conversation as we search for the best image to convey our thoughts. But private conversation is one thing; it's another when professional communicators mix their metaphors in public. Below is a selection of the best from our politicians, commentators, and the media.

Politics

Let's start with a classic, reputedly made by an 18th-century Scottish politician:

> Mr Speaker, Sir, I smell a rat, I see him floating in the air, but mark me, Sir, I will nip him in the bud.

What is it about politics and rats? Or, indeed, any metaphor that walks:

> Everything under the sun that walks on two legs and hasn't got a party of its own is in the ALP.

The author of this line was a master of mixing metaphors:

> It's no good putting a wet blanket over wages and prices, because that's only the tip of the iceberg.

In fact, Australian politics has one of the finest traditions of mixing metaphors:

> We have a situation where the signal rippling through the bamboo grapevine is that Australia is a green light.

> I will go in to bat for my fellow Australians who are going to fall off the cliff ... I am torn between two places and a hard rock.

At other times, there is an agricultural theme:

> The chickens are finally coming home to roost for a premier who's gone to sleep at the infrastructure wheel.

And the following spot of tree-fishing:

> The clock is ticking on climate change and we can't just shuffle around and hope that something falls out of the trees. We actually have to land an outcome.

Some politicians are so adept at the art that they extend their metaphor-mixing:

> If Australia's approach is manning the life rafts as the economic boat steams happily over the horizon, leaving us forlorn and destitute in an economic ocean of grief completely of our own making, then what sort of example is that to the world?

The epic mixed metaphor is ever to the ready when times are grim:

> These are big days for the nation. They are big days for the world. We're actually going through some crunch times. No-one's Robinson Crusoe. Therefore, what's required is a bit of political courage for everyone to collectively step up to the plate. We're at one of those crossover points in the world, one of those crossover points in Australia.

Or simply as a way of saying that nothing happened:

> There are dozens of sticking points on the Doha Round right now. Let's just be blunt about it. But where it was before, which was in a pre-glacial position, we are now moving rapidly down the glacier. Except, unlike most moving glaciers, we have five weeks to arrive at the end point. You know, it is going to take a bit more to gelignite this thing into gear.

The Commentariat

If you were looking to the media as a paragon of clarity, you may want to skip over this next section. When it comes to incisive analysis, the press gallery is just as prone to metaphor-mangling:

> Is the bottom-line crunch [that] there's too little jam to spread?
>
> Did you see the writing on the wall, or did the penny drop later?
>
> He has been made a sacrificial lamb for taking the lid off a can of worms.
>
> His iron rule in the end became a rod for the party's back.

Then there are spokespeople and lobbyists shaping public debate with wisdom such as:

> We need to make sure we don't stereotype students into a particular mould.
>
> [The department] is a backwater clogged with hot potatoes.
>
> This is a warning across the bows that shows that people will move in bulk.
>
> What we want across the board is a line in the sand so we can have a level playing field.

Away from the cut and thrust of the nightly news, experts have time to work up wisdom like the following:

> Once the milk has been spilt in this sort of case, it's very difficult to put Humpty Dumpty back on the wall again.
>
> It's dog eat dog in this rat race.
>
> When you are in Korea, you have to eat as the Romans do.
>
> That's the gravy on the cake.
>
> He's come on in fits and bounds.

Finally, there are always the sports commentators, who mix metaphors freely. There was a swimmer who apparently 'climbed every mountain in swimming', and a boxer who delivered 'a low blow between the belt'. We leave you with a tennis commentator, who surely wins the grand prize:

> Lleyton's a person who's on heat during a grand slam and there's not quite the stigma that surrounds Federer that there was at his peak, when he was untouchable. A few more guys have got wings, and Lleyton's just got to find a way to get in his kitchen.

EUPHEMISMS (OR YOUSE-FEMISMS)

In a society renowned for its rugged individualism, where we are supposed to call a spade a spade, we have of late got into the habit of calling it an articulated portable digging implement.

We all drop easily into euphemism as a form of politeness, such as when describing a friend as 'a bit broad in the beam' or 'rather big-boned', instead of fat. It's easier to tell kids that their pet frog has 'gone to heaven' and is now 'asleep with Jesus' than that it is dead. Euphemisms also help us talk about uncomfortable topics, such as when we are 'between jobs' or 'on gardening leave'. And there's a handy euphemism for every bodily function, whether we are blowing chunks, breaking wind, basting the ham, or buffing the banana. At Manglish HQ, we call these code-yellow euphemisms. They can be socially useful, often do little harm, and can add some colour to the language.

Then there are the code-red equivalents: euphemisms that deliberately set out to obfuscate. Governments and corporations use them to downplay something that they don't want us to think about. Advertisements become 'short breaks', a dilapidated house becomes 'a handyman's delight', and toxic debt becomes 'a legacy asset'. The military uses 'enhanced interrogation techniques', film stars employ 'gestational carriers', and the government engages in 'strategic non-communication'.

Code-yellow Euphemisms

We first pick up euphemisms as children, when those around us prefer not to talk too directly about bodily functions. We may hear these:

Call of nature

Doo-doo

Do your business

Little girls' room

Number ones

Spend a penny

Wee-wee

It's no surprise when our parents apply the same principles as we approach puberty:

BO

Calendar pains

Cramps

Nocturnal emissions

Boys, in particular, are rather shy about:

Applying the handbrake

Clearing the snorkel

Doing the one-gun salute

Shooting putty at the moon

Squeezing the toothpaste

Teaching the Cyclops the lambada

Yet rebellious teenagers are happy to boast about becoming:

Inebriated

Out of it

Tiddly

Under the weather

And how they:

Called God on the porcelain telephone

Downloaded dinner

Reviewed the day's menu

Displayed the chunky carrots

As young adults, they update those early euphemisms for doo-doos:

Chocolate thunder

Drain the radiator

Hinder blast

Lay some cable

Meadow dressing

Point Percy at the porcelain

Shake dew off the lily

Entering the workforce, others find euphemistic wit in describing their new colleagues with the following terms:

A beer short of a sixpack

A couple of sandwiches short of a picnic

Doesn't have both oars in the water

A few roos short of a top paddock

Got a mind like a steel sieve

A sausage short on the barbie

Sharp as a bowling ball

A tool short in the toolbox

For sheer creativity, however, nothing rivals the euphemisms for our genitals:

Bald-headed butler

Bearded clam

Cranny hunter

Dart of love

Family jewels

House under the hill

Nether regions

One-eyed trouser snake

Private parts

Sugar basin

Tool

Velvet-helmeted warrior

This abundance multiplies in the copious euphemisms surrounding sex:

Adult erotica

Au naturel

Bonking

Extramarital activity

Go all the way

Hide the sausage

Massage parlour

Rumpy-pumpy

Slam the clam

Slap and tickle

Soixante-neuf

Swinging

Well-hung

EXTRAMARITAL ACTIVITY

Which might be our way to avoid thinking about becoming deceased and dearly departed when we:

Cash in our chips

Draw the last breath

Drop off the perch

Expire

Get eternal rest

Go to heaven

Pass away

Code-red Euphemisms

When it comes to egregious euphemisms about death, no-one can rival the military. It's a sensitive thing, sending your population off to kill people in another country, and even more sensitive when they don't come home in one piece. So governments of all persuasions work hard to tone down the reality of their killing machines.

When soldiers returned from World War One, many suffered from 'shell shock'. We initially described this terrible condition with economy and directness. So direct, in fact, that after World War Two it was re-titled 'battle fatigue', and during the Korean War, 'operational exhaustion'. It has now transformed into 'post-traumatic stress disorder'. The condition is real and devastating; the language has gradually leached away that reality.

Our military is full of code-red euphemisms:

Active defence

Anti-personnel

Asymmetric warfare

Attrition

Casualty

Collateral damage

Deconflict

Department of Defence

Destabilise

Friendly fire

Neutralise

Pacify

Permanent pre-hostility

Strategic exchange of fire

Surgical strikes

Writer Christopher Hitchens has described what he called the 'mental and moral offense of euphemism'. Here are some of the worst examples from the war in Iraq:

Civilian security contractors
Mercenaries

Concerned local citizens
Newly bribed allies

Enhanced interrogation techniques
Torture

Ethno-sectarian conflict
Civil war

Human-caused disaster
Terrorism

Overseas contingency operation
War

Sons of Iraq
See 'Concerned local citizens'

But if warfare generates the worst obfuscation, governments are apt to apply the selfsame techniques to social problems. Towards the end of the last drought in Australia, a government report suggested that agencies replace the word 'drought' with the term 'the big dry' because that would lessen the psychological impact on struggling farmers. Fortunately, it didn't catch on, but plenty of policyspeak euphemisms have:

Callgirl

Closure

Correction centre

Developmentally delayed

Differently abled

Disadvantaged

Interfered with

Overweight

Retrenched

Sight-deprived

Underprivileged

Visually challenged

Predictably, euphemisms were also quick to emerge during the global financial crisis, when politicians adopted the initialism 'GFC' so that they could avoid saying the word 'crisis' in public. Bailouts and toxic debt conveniently became 'temporary capital assistance packages', 'liquidity backstops', and 'legacy assets'. Executives apparently did not commit fraud or lie to anyone; they were simply 'economical with the truth' and 'engaged in strategic non-communication', despite the 'on-the-ground evidence'. This caused them to issue 'erroneous reports' that contained 'questionable errata' about their commissions and contributions.

All of it first-class, code-red Manglish.

TO PC OR NOT TO PC

Lewis Carroll was onto something in *Through the Looking-glass* when Humpty Dumpty argued:

> When I use a word ... it means just what I choose it to mean — neither more nor less.

The logic could apply perfectly to political correctness, for few concepts about language have drawn such wildly opposing views.

Talk to anyone of a progressive bent, and political correctness is simply the respectful use of neutral language that won't offend others. PC expressions replace words that reveal a bias about gender, race, or ability:

Man the stall
Staff the stall

Policeman
Police officer

Black
Aboriginal, African, or African-American person

Skip
Anglo-Australian person

Handicapped
Person with a disability

Spastic
Person with cerebral palsy

The term 'political correctness' itself dates back to the 18th century, but it gained prominence in the 1980s as an ironic in-joke among those on the left who recognised that it could be taken too far. In the United States, for example, there were attempts to ban Coon cheese because of the brandname's association with an offensive word for African people. The manufacturer defended its brand on eponymous grounds, given that an Edward W. Coon actually invented the Cooning process for maturing cheese quickly.

Examples like this prompted warriors of the political right to take up their cudgels and turn political correctness into a term of derision, labelling it the worst attempt at thought control since the Soviet Union at the height of the Cold War. Definitions of political correctness at this end of the spectrum can get colourful:

A law of moral and ethical relativism that pretends that we are all equal

A way of speaking so we don't offend whining pussies

The new communism … attempting to control our thoughts

So when exactly is political correctness justified, and when does it verge into Manglish?

To PC

Language reflects society, so it's hardly surprising that, as social structures change, there will be pressure to change the way in which we describe them. As we improved the status of women, for example, it was inevitable that the use of the word 'man' to represent both genders would come under fire. And we can easily turn the 'man in the street' to the 'person in the street', and 'mankind' into 'humankind', and the 'average man' into 'the average person'. A line like the following would not even be scientifically consistent:

The development of the uterus in rats, guinea pigs, and men

Job titles have proved readily adaptable to recognise that men are no longer the only workers in a range of occupations:

Chairman
Chairperson/Chair

Authoress
Author

Salesman
Salesperson

Spokesman
Spokesperson

We can also avoid qualifications that have little relevance to a person's ability to do a job:

Dr Smith, the prominent Jewish politician

An outstanding woman golfer

A leading black historian

And it is hard to argue against political correctness where a term would genuinely cause offence, such as with racial slurs:

Boong

Spic

Wog

Not to PC

At the same time, the PC brigade can and does get carried away, particularly when it seeks to ban a usage that has no connection with a coincidentally offensive word. In Australia, for example, a Santa school tried to replace the words 'ho, ho, ho' with 'ha, ha, ha' because the word 'ho' also happens to be slang for a prostitute. It didn't take on.

In the United States, one Washington bureaucrat nearly lost his job after he used the term 'niggardly' in a speech to describe a budget measure. He was saved only when a dictionary showed everyone the word had no connection to the word 'nigger'.

And a few years ago, a kindergarten chain in the United Kingdom changed the words of *Baa, Baa, Black Sheep* to 'baa, baa, rainbow sheep' in case the traditional words reinforced racial stereotypes. No matter that the original rhyme was actually a political allegory about taxation. Or that 'baa, baa, rainbow sheep' is surely a crime against poetry, given that it doesn't even scan.

The list goes on. The expression 'a chink in the armour' has been challenged because of its association with the derogatory word for a Chinese person. Some organisations suggest that their staff have 'thought showers' instead of 'brainstorming' meetings in case they offend people with epilepsy. *The Times* reported a raft of terms that public-sector organisations were trying to remove from their language:

Black day
Miserable day

Gentlemen's agreement
Unwritten agreement

Right-hand man
Second-in-command

To PC or Not to PC?

Manglish can exist at either end of the PC spectrum. There is certainly a case for replacing genuinely offensive words. But blindly replacing anything that might have the vaguest connection to an offensive term can undermine the entire exercise.

Our biggest challenge is that the middle ground is constantly shifting. We will always struggle with words that relate to difficult social problems. Any term we choose can take on negative connotations, no matter how well intended it was at the time. So we change it again.

Following are two examples of how PC terms have shifted over the decades. First, as the social status of African-Americans improved, the words used to describe them changed significantly:

Coloured

Negro

Black

Afro-American

African-American

And people with disabilities have been through a similar shift in name:

Crippled

Handicapped

Disabled person

Person with a disability

In each generation, the people coining these words thought they had finally nailed it – at last, here were the words representing neutral ground. But we should remember Humpty Dumpty: our words mean precisely what we choose them to mean. When a political ground is contested, the language describing it is seldom stable.

POLLIE WAFFLE

No account of modern Manglish would be complete without a quick look at the language of politics. At the end of the day, moving forwards, only a parliament can provide the extensive training required to master the Manglish of pollie waffle.

Pollie Filler

The first type of pollie waffle is prominent at press conferences and doorstop interviews, where politicians need to buy time to think about what not to say. They delay any kind of response with 'pollie filler' – meaningless words and phrases such as:

At the end of the day

At this particular moment/point in time

The challenge is

Going forwards

Having said that

I'm glad you asked that question

In terms of

It's been the stated objective

Look, um, er

Moving forwards

Obviously

Thank you for your question

That's a very good question

The truth of the matter is

To be honest

Um, er, look

With all due respect

Without a word of a lie

You know

Pollies also buy thinking time throughout an interview by using the interviewer's first name endearingly, ad nauseam, and completely without need:

There's only one poll that counts, [insert interviewer's first name].

We don't respond to hypothetical questions, [insert interviewer's first name].

We never speculate about that, [insert interviewer's first name].

We're not interested in opinion polls, [insert interviewer's first name].

It's almost as if their interviewers are amnesiacs and will forget their own names unless they get helpful and regular reminders. Yet the real purpose is to fill out the allotted time without answering a question.

And when it comes to avoiding a question, nothing rivals this all-time press-conference classic from a secretary of defence in the United States:

Reports that say that something hasn't happened are always interesting to me because as we know, there are known knowns; there are things we know we know. We also know there are known unknowns; that is to say we know there are some things we do not know. But there are also unknown unknowns — the ones we don't know we don't know.

Classic Australian Pollie Waffle

Speaking of the classics, it may have been some decades now since a certain Queensland premier left office, but his linguistic legacy lingers. No account of pollie waffle would be complete without gems such as:

We're moving in all directions at once.

I'm only telling you as I see the situation. I am steeped in politics backwards.

His defence of human rights was legendary:

We intend to uphold the rights of the individual. If they want to march up Queen Street, disrupt all the traffic, stop the legitimate comings and goings of people, we simply won't let them do it.

As was his vision for the environment:

Moreton Island will be rehabilitated after the mining people have been there in such a way you won't recognise it.

But the zenith of his wisdom has to be:

Who wants to stick together with them and get your feet wet? You know, if you get stick foot on sticky paper, you get both of them on, you fall over and Mr Hawke asks us to stick with him. You put your foot on this sticky with him, his and Keating, his government's got their feet on sticky paper, my word they have.

To which we can only conclude:

Nothing has been decided yet; don't let's jump to confusions.

Of course, pollie waffle is an entirely bipartisan phenomenon, and thrives in every party in every state in every country. A minister of a different political persuasion announced:

We have torn up the verbal agreement.

Those verbal agreements just aren't worth the paper they are written on anymore. Mind you, it took a British minister to come up with this warning:

If you open up that Pandora's box you never know what Trojan horses will jump out.

An Australian trade minister explained:

They're moving things around the different baskets, but it will be the end game in terms of putting numbers in square brackets in terms of tariff reductions, if there's significant requests on time frames in terms of phase-in.

A health minister replied:

It's very clear, I think, from the totality of the opposition's question, and the totality of the prime minister's answer, exactly what the context of the answer was.

And a roads minister clarified:

At the end of the day, it's everyone's responsibility to slow down and drive safely.

It seems that at other times of the day it's perfectly okay to speed.

Contemporary Classics

Lest we start feeling smug about former politicians, recent times have presented some pretty rich pollie waffle. For a while, it seemed that no prime ministerial statement was complete without a sprinkling of acronyms and diplomatic jargon to demonstrate foreign-policy experience:

> So, rather than add to the alphabet soup which already exists, my own predisposition is that it's far better to grow real security-related work, for example, out of the ARF. That I think of itself begins to construct de facto if not de jure for the sort of competence in security-building measures which evolve institutionally through things like the CSCE process in Europe.

The following answer sent the translators in Germany reaching for their dictionaries:

> It is highly unlikely that anything will emerge from the MEF in terms of detailed programmatic specificity.

Meanwhile, in Washington, Australia's fearless prime minister explained his country's evolving relationship with China:

> There is ... on the face of it a natural complementarity between the two philosophical approaches, and a complementarity that could be developed further in the direction of some form of conceptual synthesis.

While his successor as prime minister was overseas, the opposition was busy spouting some rolled-gold pollie waffle of its own about why a tax is not a tax:

> Well, we don't call it a tax, we're calling it an investment in human capital.

The leader of the opposition then got a little too honest about which core and non-core promises represent gospel truth:

> I know politicians are going to be judged on everything they say, but sometimes, in the heat of discussion, you go a little bit further than you would if it was an absolutely calm, considered, prepared, scripted remark, which is one of the reasons why the statements that need to be taken absolutely as gospel truth is [sic] those carefully prepared, scripted remarks.

Which perhaps explains why the subsequent election turned into a campaign of the ventriloquist dummies, with both candidates spouting tightly scripted, focus-group-driven, 'on-message' drivel:

> Our great nation, our very great nation, has been built by generations of men and women who had the courage to move forward.

As opposed to those shit-scared men and women with time machines who all went backward.

LEGAL(UN)ESE AND COPTALK

They say that ignorance is no excuse for breaking the law. But why do they make the law so hard to understand? Imagine that you are a farmer, for example, trying to make sense of what the following lemon means for your own fruit:

> The provision of sections 43 and 48 shall with such modifications as are necessary extend and apply to and in relation to this Division and, without affecting the generality of the foregoing, in particular with the modifications, that ... a reference to eggs or egg products shall be construed as a reference to citrus fruit.

Translation, anyone? How about:

> What sections 43 and 48 say about eggs and egg products will also apply to citrus fruits.

Legal(un)ese

Lawyers argue that they have to write in such a longwinded way to make their meaning precise. They elaborate because they wrestle with the noble task of certainty. Given that other lawyers will prod and probe at their text to twist it into unintended meanings, they couldn't possibly write something straightforward, such as:

> I will send you a dozen red roses.

After all, there might be an obscure 16th-century case in the Lower Snug local court which ruled that 'a dozen' could also mean 13. So they forestall that possibility by writing:

> I will send you a total amount of not fewer than but not exceeding one dozen red roses consisting of twelve (12) roses.

And lest we be unclear about what we mean by a red rose:

> I will send you a total amount of not fewer than but not exceeding one dozen red roses consisting of twelve (12) roses consisting of stems of approximately 12 inches in length with thorns present along the stem at regular intervals and petals of the appearance of the colour red.

All that remains is to specify what we mean by 'give' and we have a perfect piece of legal precision:

> The present author will provide by conveyances including but not limited to post courier pony express and registered delivery a total amount of not fewer than but not exceeding one dozen red roses consisting of twelve (12) roses consisting of stems of approximately 12 inches in length with thorns present along the stem at regular intervals and petals of the appearance of the colour red.

Notice that it's all interconnected, so it can't be divided into separate sentences. It doesn't contain any of that newfangled punctuation, either.

An exaggeration? Here's a sample from a real contract:

> The Consultant will ensure that the Specified Personnel undertake work in respect of the Services in accordance with the terms of this Agreement and will not be hindered or prevented in any way in the performance of their duties in carrying out the Services including but not limited to being removed from the performance of the Services or being requested to perform services which in any way interfere with the due performance of the Services by the Specified Personnel.

Maybe that was only supposed to be read by another lawyer, and they all get off on this stuff. But how about this, from the terms and conditions of a ferry ticket:

> The TT-Line reserves the right at any time to substitute one vessel for another to abandon or alter any voyage either before the commencement or at any time during the course thereof to dispatch the vessel before or after the date or hour advertised or announced for her sailing from any port to deviate from any advertised route for any purpose with liberty to sail without pilots, to proceed via any route, to proceed, return to and stay at any ports whatsoever (including the loading port) in any order in or out of the route or in contrary direction to or beyond the port of destination ...

This is only the first part of a 204-word virtually unpunctuated sentence, in a document that rambles on for five very dense pages.

It boils down to something like this: 'Well, you might have a ticket, but we don't actually have to take you anywhere at the time it says.' While that's annoying, at least it stops you from worrying over what it might mean to head 'in contrary direction to or beyond the port of destination', particularly if the company takes up its 'liberty to sail without pilots'.

Coptalk

While legalese is frustrating when wielded by lawyers, it reaches its peak when non-lawyers in the justice system give it a go. There's no better example than the euphemistic language that police use. A police officer recalling a crime will never say something like:

> Police entered the house and found two dead people in the front room. They then saw a man running from the back of the house and arrested him after a short chase.

They go to great pains to turn their text into coptalk:

> Officers gained entry into the residence whereupon two deceased persons were located in the room immediately adjacent to the street. The officers proceeded to the rear of the premises and observed a male person moving rapidly in an easterly direction from the building. The officers undertook

a pursuit of short duration, after which a male person was apprehended and is helping police with their inquiries.

Coptalk takes years of careful training at the academy, where they learn to replace clear words with vague euphemisms and legal jargon, such as the following:

Apprehended
Arrested

Assailant
Attacker

Deceased persons
Dead people

Domestic disturbance
Fight or argument

Exchanged greetings
Said hello

Fatality
Death

Infringement notice
Fine

It was advised that
Police were told

Juvenile or minor
Child or teenager

Male person or female person
Man or woman

Observe
See

Person of light-skinned appearance
A light-skinned person

Person of interest
Suspect

Person who may be able to assist police with their investigations
Suspect

Proceeded to the vicinity of
Went to

Taken into custody
Arrested

Whereabouts unknown
Missing

PERSON OF DISINTEREST

The most painful coptalk is the tangle that police get into when they talk about unpleasant things such as rape or murder. Some euphemism is understandable here, but the temptation for police is to leach all life out of their language when it is convenient to do so. For example:

The officer deployed a taser, causing the man to comply with directions.

Another officer was asked to explain his actions in a courtroom:

Officer: I attempted to apply an escort hold to the subject, but I noted resistive tension in his arm, so I applied pain compliance instead. The subject actively resisted, so I administered a focused knee strike to the lower abdominal area, and decentralised the subject.

Lawyer: In other words, Officer, you tried to grab my client's arm, and when he pulled away you twisted his wrist, and then kicked him in the groin and threw him down on the pavement, is that about it?

Then there is this classic line about a police officer bitten on the genitals by a ferret he was 'escorting' back to a wildlife refuge:

The ferret got itself out of the box and latched itself to a place of undesirable intent on the police officer's person.

Rumour has it that the children of police are schooled in this argot from an early age so that they can converse with their parents. We have it on good authority that what follows is a real extract from *The Young Policeperson's Bumper Book of Nursery Rhymes*:

A child or young person answering to the name of Muffet
Was observed in proximity to a tuffet
In the act of consuming produce described as curds and whey
Whereupon it is alleged that an offender of the appearance of
  a spider
Loitered in a malicious manner in the vicinity of said juvenile
Causing her to proceed rapidly from the premises in an
  agitated way.

LOST IN TRANSLATION

You can always count on the boys in blue to complicate a diplomatic visit. Police in Australia settled on 'Blue Gum' as the codename for the task of protecting President Obama during his first trip Down Under. Why this kind of operation had to be given a codename in the first place is a question all to itself. But by choosing 'Blue Gum', the hapless plods unerringly chose an offensive slang term for a lazy African-American worker. Not the most diplomatic words to greet that country's first African-American president.

Of course, the police were merely continuing one of the finest international traditions: getting lost in translation. Politicians are particularly adept at waltzing into another country and sticking their feet into foreign mouths, and the corporate sector is not far behind.

The Political Classics

According to retired diplomat Richard Woolcott, when an Australian diplomat was speaking Mandarin in China, he interpreted their countries' close relationship in this way:

> Australia and China are enjoying simultaneous orgasms in their relationship.

He was emulating a previous prime minister, who had once assured the Japanese parliament that union leaders would 'not play funny buggers with you'. The Japanese leadership was told that the unions:

> Won't play laughing homosexuals with you.

Australia's leaders have merely been catching up to the fine translation achievements of American presidents. Jimmy Carter once wrestled with an admirable sentiment when he tried to say in Polish, 'I have a strong desire to know the Polish people.' Instead, he said:

> I desire the Polish people carnally.

Vice-president Dan Quayle didn't even need a foreign language to fall down a linguistic ravine. When touring Latin America, he lamented:

> I wish I had studied more Latin at school.

Then there was George W. Bush, who had great trouble at times remembering which country he was in and what language was spoken there. When in Sydney for an APEC summit, he thanked his hosts from 'Austria'. On a separate occasion, after catching the eye of the Italian prime minister, he called out 'Amigo! Amigo!' in Spanish.

Corporate Mistranslations

Not far behind our political elite in the translation stakes is the corporate sector. The suits on the 61st floor are often so certain about their marketing that they rarely consider how it will translate into another language.

Mitsubishi found that they had a problem when they started to market their popular four-wheel-drive vehicles in South America. In Spanish, the slang meaning of 'pajero' is 'one who practices onanism'. You can imagine the advertisement:

Please consider
The all-new
Mitsubishi Wanker

Then there was the Clairol 'mist stick', a curling iron marketed directly into Germany using its English name. Executives scratched their heads over sales until someone pointed out that 'mist' is a German slang term for manure.

The Scandinavian company Electrolux didn't factor in American slang when it marketed its vacuum cleaners with the slogan 'Nothing sucks like an Electrolux.'

But the first prize in corporate mistranslations goes to American Airlines for marketing the perks of flying business class with the phrase 'Vuelo en Cuero', or 'fly in leather'. In Mexican Spanish, this also means 'fly in the nude'.

It's the Idiom, Idiot

The underlying cause of many mistranslations is the use of idiom: metaphors that are understood by the speakers of one language, but have a very different literal meaning in another. For example:

English: The spirit is willing but the flesh is weak
Russian: The vodka is good but the meat is spoiled

English: Come alive with the Pepsi generation
Chinese: Pepsi brings back your dead ancestors

Multiple translations of an idiomatic phrase never fail to amuse:

English: To have your cake and eat it too
Japanese: Because it has the cake and for the sake of you eat
French: Since it arranges the cake and eats for you
Italian: Since it comes to an agreement and it stops in you eats the cake

English: Fair shake of the sauce bottle
Japanese: Fair treatment of sauce bottle
Chinese: Sauce bottle's fair play
German: Appropriate vibration of the sauce flask

The Hidden Beauty of Engrish

Fortunately, getting lost in translation isn't solely the province of English-speakers. The most twisted examples come from Engrish, a form of Manglish that takes on haiku-like qualities when used on clothing, signs, and food packaging throughout Asia. There was this, on a packet of tissues:

My Wet
Cool & Refreshing
Tissue for New Life

A closed ticket-office window helpfully advised:

You are available at next ticket office.
Thank you.

Before a toilet sign clarified where to go:

Lavatory
It has separated to the male and the woman.
Don't mistake.

In a gift shop, a T-shirt selectively excerpted these words from an English pop song, giving them an entirely new spin:

Future voices
need to be heard.
Eyebrows are always.

And a child's bib proclaimed:

Capsule children
Very wonderfully and more pleasantly.

Visiting a temple is a solemn occasion, so:

Please do not see it while drinking drink.
The PET bottle caps it and put it in a bag, and please carry it.
Please see the thing which the chief does not have after finishing drinking.

But it takes a packet of biscuits to reach a truly poetic note:

Choco cakes
As for beautiful harmony to play,
it is probably to reflect it elegantly
this chocolate cake
your tea time.

If only 'Operation Blue Gum' had such a poetic ring.

FANCY-PANTS JOB TITLES

There once was a time when a job was simply a job. Many common jobs, in fact, became surnames: Butcher and Baker, Thatcher and Miller. Job titles generally used one word and everyone had a fair idea of the work involved.

But in the age of Manglish, clarity of occupation is anything but a virtue. That might mean workers actually understand what their managers are supposed to do. So instead, we have the Head of Technical Competence, the Career Alternative Enhancement Program Coordinator, and the Principal Business Process Analyst (but never, of course, the Secondary Business Process Analyst). What do any of these people actually do?

The trend has become so popular that it is now extending to the titles of jobs that we've had under control for centuries. We are no longer content, it seems, to be mere window cleaners when there is the prospect of becoming Vision Clearance Engineers. And how can an ordinary receptionist compete with the Head of Verbal Communications?

It's time to stop the fancy-pants nonsense before it starts to infect our surnames. Otherwise we'll be looking in the phone book for our mates Mr Leavened Foodstuffs Consultant, Ms Domicile Weatherproofing Engineer, and Mrs Animal Alimentation Providore. If that sounds far-fetched, have a look at what we've already lost.

Civil Enforcement Officer
Police officer

Customer Experience Executive
Salesperson

Customer Service Representative
Salesperson

Destination Counsellor
Travel agent

Director of First Impressions
Receptionist

Environmental Health Officer
Pest controller

Loss Prevention Officer
Security guard

Patient Care Assistant
Nurse

CIVIL ENFORCEMENT OFFICER

Qualified Unskilled Personnel
Politician

Okay, we made up that last one. But we didn't make up the rest, nor the following job titles that people have encountered in the United Kingdom:

Coin Facilitation Engineer
Tollbooth collector

Crockery Cleansing Operative
Dishwasher

Dispatch Service Facilitator
Postal worker

Domestic Engineer
Housewife/Househusband

Education Centre Nourishment Assistant
Lunch lady

Environment Improvement Technician
Cleaner

Flueologist
Chimney sweep

Foot Health Gain Facilitator
Chiropodist

Knowledge Navigator
Teacher

Media Distribution Officer
Paper boy or girl

Petroleum Transfer Engineer
Petrol station attendant

Revenue Protection Officer
Ticket inspector

Space Consultant
Real-estate agent

Stock Replenishment Adviser
Shelf stacker

Technical Horticultural Maintenance Officer
Gardener

Vision Clearance Engineer
Window cleaner

Waste Removal Engineer/Garbologist
Garbage collector

Wastewater Treatment Officer
Sewage worker

Of course, none of these comes close to the doublespeak used for people who sack the staff:

Career Change Executive

Career Alternative Enhancement Program Coordinator

Mobility Pool Manager

Vocational Relocation Consultant

Fancy-pants Job Ads

Once you get into the habit of fancy-pantsing a title, there's no stopping the job ad, either. Anyone working as an adviser or an analyst must now ensure the delivery of highly effective outcome-focused services and provide timely advice on emerging issues and developing priorities in order to liaise with key stakeholders to facilitate key projects that broker outcomes responsive to business requirements.

We used to call those 'managers'. But now they get a fancy-pants makeover:

> This position is responsible for leading a team that develops IT infrastructure architectures that ensure maximum horizontal and vertical integration of infrastructures, re-usability of IT investments, avoidance of duplication in infrastructure solutions and efficient, effective, and customer-focused delivery of IT infrastructures.

If that's what the team does, what does the position actually do? If you are not sure, you might need to employ a Channel and Brand Manager with:

> A key focus moving forward in developing a proactive approach to both internal and external customers, providing a high level of interface and support at a strategic level and delivering communications solutions that are part of the long-term planning process.
>
> To succeed in this challenging and high-impact role, you will need to be an astute and strategic leader who can deal with ambiguity.

Fancy-pants Job-title Generator

In the end, if we can't beat 'em, we will be forced to join 'em. So if you are not satisfied with your own job title, use the job-title generator on the next page and come up with a new one. All this takes is three simple steps:

1. Choose your industry sector from the first column.
2. Choose an action that vaguely relates to what you do.
3. Pick the type of title that sounds the most impressive.

Put the three together and voila! Not satisfied with being a tour guide? How about a Recreation Facilitation Consultant?

A bit miffed at being a builder? Surely you can become a Construction Progression Facilitator? And there's no need to feel depressed about being a teacher when you can become an Education Improvement Executive.

Industry	**Action**	**Title**
Legal	Discharge	Director
Health	Facilitation	Exporter
Engineering	Review	Technician
Recreation	Distribution	Provider
Utility	Renewal	Consultant
Communications	Logistics	Supplier
Management	Resourcing	Officer
Retail	Servicing	Operator
Education	Delivery	Engineer
Finance	Production	Manager
Construction	Engagement	Facilitator
Administration	Replenishment	Counsellor
Agricultural	Improvement	Assistant
Entertainment	Liaison	Executive
Technology	Cultivation	Adviser
Environmental	Generation	Specialist
Transport	Progression	Mentor
Information	Development	Custodian
Corporate	Execution	Liaison
Government	Implementation	Impresario
Industrial	Processing	Representative
Property	Enhancement	Worker
Food and Beverage	Support	Coordinator
Arts	Reengineering	Inspirator

WORLD'S WORST MISSION STATEMENTS

The military recently discovered a great new anti-interrogation technique for soldiers caught behind enemy lines. If asked about their 'mission', they can skip the usual name, rank, and serial number, and go straight to gobbledygook:

> **Our mission is to apply best practice scenarios utilising military brickware in order to facilitate optimal conflict outcomes on a fully integrated basis.**

Mission statements originated in the military, but spread quickly into government circles before finding a home in the corporate world. Today, no self-respecting company would think about setting itself up without defining its mission, its vision, and its values. It's just that most of them do it so badly.

The Overinflated

The first candidates for the world's worst mission statements are organisations that believe an overinflated style will sound intelligent and authoritative. Any idea what this organisation does?

> We provide a community engagement and dialogue clearinghouse to provide capacity training and resources to build individual and collective skills and knowledge in small- and large-scale engagement and dialogue processes.

No, we didn't make that up. That's the mission of a business that helps government agencies to talk to people. Sorry, facilitate engagement in meaningful dialogue processes with individual stakeholders.

It is not surprising that the worst offenders are the consultants who, since the early 1990s, have charged a veritable fortune to brainwash unsuspecting organisations into believing that they can't function without overinflated dot points of purpose. It is a corporate re-run of the emperor's new clothes. No-one was game to question ubiquitous lunacy such as this:

> a global network of enterprise acceleration centres that spur the growth of entrepreneurial solutions to the challenges of sustainable development. Our vision is a new, recognised asset class, comprised of entrepreneurs whose primary intent is generating positive impacts on the environment and society, backed up by a vibrant marketplace and a robust ecosystem of support.

The Vague and Useless

It's no wonder the mission statements of corporations are becoming so vague that they bear little relationship to what a company actually does. Here are some lines from three mission statements quoted by *The New York Times*. Can you tell which organisations they come from?

> ... help people and businesses throughout the world to realise their full potential

> Be the best in the eyes of our customers, employees, and stakeholders.

> Bringing the best to everyone we touch, and being the best in everything we do.

The organisations? Microsoft, American Standard, and the Estée Lauder Companies.

So if you need to tick the box and write a mission statement for your own start-up, save yourself the time and expense of a corporate-planning retreat by picking something generic from an existing statement:

> To drive sustainable growth through the power of our people and brands by better serving the needs of our consumers, customers, and communities.

If you need something longer, take this one, from a Fortune 500 retailer:

> We will constantly strive to implement the critical initiatives required to achieve our vision. In doing this, we will deliver operational excellence in every corner of the company and meet or exceed our commitments to the many constituencies we serve. All of our long-term strategies and short-term actions will be moulded by a set of core values that are shared by each and every associate.

The Self-evident

A more insidious aspect of the mission statement is the way in which it is moving into areas that have a pretty self-evident purpose. One public school recently felt the need to capture its mission as providing:

> quality education for all students in a supportive and challenging environment characterised by excellent teaching/learning programs, a caring and professional staff, and involved parents and community.

What else is a school for but to educate?

Hospitals are also embracing these absurd statements of the obvious:

> The Mission Statement of the St George Hospital and Community Health Service is 'Good Health Care — Better Health'.

A hospital is hardly likely to have the mission of making people sick, is it?

Now even churches are getting in on the act. One describes (part) of its mission as:

> To reach and influence the world by building a large Christ-centred, Bible-based church, changing mindsets and empowering people to lead and impact in every sphere of life.

But the apotheosis of the obvious is the trend to write 'family' and 'individual' mission statements. Websites encourage us to sit down as a family unit and write down our 'values and goals'. Career advisers urge candidates to include a 'personal mission statement' that captures their life mission to work for a particular organisation. As this is seldom the reality, these are so general that they become meaningless:

My personal mission is to work for an organisation that values my skills and experience, and will allow me to work as part of a team environment to develop professionally and enjoy future opportunities.

The Hypocritical

Yet the winners, undoubtedly, of the world's worst mission statements are those major corporations that capture an ideal they don't live up to. There was a major bank that went belly up, leaving administrators with the following hollow statement:

To be a specialised lending and savings bank which aims to deliver superior value to customers and shareholders through excellent products, efficiency, and growth.

Then there is the (ongoing) mission of the oil company that brought us the worst spill in history:

We help the world meet its growing need for heat, light, and mobility. And we strive to do that by producing energy that is affordable, secure, and doesn't damage the environment.

At other times, mission statements resort to Manglish when they can't be too honest about their corporate interests. Here's the mission of a pizza chain:

> Our aim is to change the perception of pizza for all our customers, taking away the guilt factor, bringing the enjoyment back to eating takeaway food, giving our customers options regarding their health, and most of all creating a great-tasting product.

And the winner? It's hard to go past the giant tobacco company that describes two of the four strategies that make up its mission:

> Align with Society: We will actively participate in resolving societal concerns that are relevant to our business.
>
> Satisfy Adult Consumers: We will convert our deep understanding of adult tobacco consumer needs into better, more creative, and more satisfying products.

We guess they can't come out and say that their mission is to make us all smoke more.

STRAYAN, NEW ZILLUND, AND YANKSPEAK

This book is generally about the use and abuse of language, rather than the accent we do it in. But at times, accents can and do cause confusion.

Strayan and New Zillund Accents

Victorians (more so Melburnians) have a propensity to swap the 'el' sound in speech for an 'al' sound, and vice versa. Melbourne thus becomes Malburn, Alfred becomes Elfred, television becomes talavision, and helicopter becomes hali-copter. Elton and Elvis transform into Alton and Alvis, Ellis becomes Alice, and the El Alamein fountain becomes Al Elamein fountain. Malburnians are therefore advised not to name their sons Allen or their daughters Ellen if these children are ever likely to cross the border or appear on national quiz shows.

Naturally, none of the Victorian readers of this book speaks like that, and it is true that some of the broadest Australian accents emanate from New South Wales and Queensland.

In states proud of their convict-free ancestry, the accent has developed due to the influence of postwar English migrants. South Australians (and sometimes Western Australians) often elongate 'no' into something that sounds like 'noee' or 'noyee', and have a propensity to swallow their Ls, just like:

Myrtwle, the schoowlgirwl from Glenewlg who won the gowld medawl in the hurdwles.

Of course, across the Tasman we have the land of the dis-emvowelled. Struggling to communicate with only 21 letters in their alphabet, the New Zillund accent frequently gives rise to misunderstandings, sometimes with amusing consequences. Hill becomes hull, this is thus, and that is thet. Pigs are found on clothes lines, you receive a bull after your meal, tin comes after nine, guess is what we cook with, and the ear is what we breathe. Ask New Zillunders what they do about sex at night and they normally respond, 'We have dunner.' And passengers arriving at any airport in New Zillund (Airn Zaird) are encouraged to proceed to the 'big chicken'. That's where they chicken their bigs.

The final score: Straya sucks, New Zillund sairvun. And that, our fallow Strayans and New Zillunders, is enough about our accents!

Yankspeak

While differences in accent are even more pronounced when we cross the Pacific, American and Australian English often combine to produce something completely foreign to comprehensible English. We have decided to give it a name: Yankspeak.

This language is creeping insidiously into the Australian and New Zealand idiom. It is no longer rare to hear sentences without a verb, or sentences that have left out important words and added superfluous ones. Or nouns turned into verbs and verbs into nouns, or sentences without subjects, and participles with a life of their own. And sentences in which adjectives are asked to do the work of adverbs.

If you are in the United States and your pilot tells you that 'we'll be taking off momentarily', it does not mean that you're about to crash or that you'll soon need to 'de-plane'. He means that we'll be taking off 'in a moment'. He just doesn't know the difference.

Similarly, a 'fanny' in the United States is a backside, bottom, or bum. A fanny pack is a bum bag. However, in Australia and New Zealand, 'fanny' means 'vagina'. So Australian and New Zealand women can rightly be extremely perplexed if skiing in the United States and confronted with the sign, 'Turn your fanny pack around to the front.'

Probably the most irritating Yankspeak to invade our idiom is the misuse, abuse, and utter overuse of the word 'like'. Normally a verb, it's now the new 'um' and 'er' (or perhaps, more precisely, 'd'oh' or 'der'). Most American teenagers can barely utter a sentence, let alone a phrase or clause, without a liberal sprinkling of 'like'. Worse, the verb 'to say' has now been universally replaced by the verb 'to go'. Combined, we end up with such Neanderthal utterances as:

He went, I'm like, wow, and she goes, like, you know, I'm like, outta here.

Such misuse can have a number of effects, including chronic depression and cerebral haemorrhage, so be careful. You may want to pause halfway through the following list of Yankspeak. Have a coffee. Take a walk. Make a right. Do dinner. Lay down. Go to the bathroom. Before it all gets on top of you.

Aluminum
Aluminium

A-okay
All right

Appetiser
Entree

Ass
Arse (or donkey ...)

Bad-ass
Tough and intimidating

Bathroom
Lavatory or toilet

Buddy
Mate

Bummer
A bad thing

Butt
Arse

Can or john
Toilet

Car trunk
Car boot

Cockamamie
Crazy or stupid

Coop
Coupé

Cooten
Couldn't

De-plane
Get off an aeroplane

Ditten
Didn't

Do dinner
Have dinner

Do the math
Do the maths

Drug
Dragged

Dude
Bloke

Dumb-ass
Idiot

Exact same thing
Exactly the same thing

Get-go
Start

Get off of (e.g. a bus)
Get off (e.g. a bus)

Gratuity
Compulsory service fee

Have a nice day
Goodbye

He dove into the pool
He dived into the pool

He's bad news
He's trouble

Honey, I shrunk the kids
Honey, I shrank the kids

Hood
Bonnet

If you will
If you like

I'll come by your house
I'll come to your house

I'll write you
I'll write to you

TRUNK

I'm done
I'm finished

In back of
Behind

Inside of/outside of
Inside/outside

Ketchup
Tomato sauce

Labratory
Laboratory

Lay down
Lie down

Make a right
Turn right

Momentarily
In a moment

No can do
Sorry, I can't

One hundred sixty-two
One hundred and sixty-two

Pissed
Angry

Poop
Crap

Right here/right there/right now
Here/there/now

Rooting for you
Barracking for you

Take care
Goodbye

Takeout
Takeaway

Totally awesome
Amazing

Touch base
Make contact

Tracheotomy
Tracheostomy

A ways down the road
A good distance away

A whole bunch
A lot

Wooten
Wouldn't

Zilch
Nothing

SPAKFILLA

While we justifiably oppose the invasive Manglish of Yank-speak, it's worth noting that Australians and New Zealanders have a range of their own linguistic foibles. In casual conversation, we like to confuse visitors by naming things with words that have the opposite meaning. Someone called 'Bluey' or 'Blue' is invariably a man with red hair. 'Shorty' is at least six-feet, three-inches tall. If a tradie responds with 'no worries' as you explain a problem, you can expect trouble. If he or she says 'no wuckers', it's definitely time to panic.

The worst examples tend to involve Spakfilla, a linguistic variant of DIY putty. This consists of several forms of phatic speech that we use to render our sentences, without adding anything of value.

Finishing a Sentence

To begin with, Australians have a unique habit of answering their own questions in the same sentence. This presupposes that the person to whom the question is addressed is either deaf, dumb, or both. How many times have you heard the following?

> How ya gowen ... good?
>
> Where've ya been ... at the footy?

What's for tea ... chops?

How was Wellington ... windy?

These questions are also complemented by a rising tone. An upward inflection is common in Australia, particularly in Queensland and among the young. It suggests uncertainty, and possibly apology, and shows no signs of waning.

Strayans and Kiwis also add a word or two at the end of a sentence, even when making a statement. The uninitiated may take this to be a gratuitous insult, but it is in fact a sign of endearment. Here are a few examples you may recognise.

And that

Ay/eh

But

Like

Okay

Right

Ya know

Yeah-no

This all leads to that pinnacle of a sentence, ending:

... yeah-no, like, ya know and that, but, ay, right?

Verbal Spakfilla

Our art of the superfluous word is hardly confined to the end of a sentence. Speak with anyone who is concentration-deprived, and you will have to dig out their meaning from underneath a thick palette of verbal Spakfilla. This is especially prominent during the teenage years. Here are some examples:

Arr

Kind of, like

Pretty much

Umm

Whatever

Ya know

Put these together and you get what passes for conversation among 16-year-olds. Here's just one exchange overheard on a train:

So I was like, you know, kind of, um, pretty much, what do you mean?

Yeah-no, then she said, ya know, arr, like, whatever.

But before we are accused of, like, discriminating against the yoof of today, it is worth noting that adults are equally adept at Spakfilla. They are just better at disguising it.

The Australian political classes have particular need of words and phrases devoid of meaning so that they can fill in a sound bite or give themselves time to think up even worse Manglish. One minister was dubbed 'Mr In-Relation-To' because of his constant stream of prepositional Spakfilla. After all, what's the point of using one word when you can use four or five?

by way of
as, by

for the purpose of
for

in order to
to

in relation to
about, for, to, so

in such a way that
so

in terms of
for

in the case of
if

until such time as
until

with regards to
about, for, to, so

with respect to
about, for, to, so

Put these together, as Mr In-Relation-To regularly did, and you can answer any question in Manglish and leave no meaning behind:

In terms of the matters raised in relation to the question with regard to this issue, it is important to note that it may not be possible to reply for the purposes of an answer until such time as the department is in a position in order to provide advice by way of background.

More recently, a prime minister has managed to disguise her personal Spakfilla in two otherwise-innocent words: 'look' and 'obviously'. These are always prominent when she is answering a difficult question:

Look, obviously my focus today is on attending this event, although obviously I will be pursuing this. But look, this will obviously have to wait for another day.

Other Phatic Forms

But before most of us get to the conversational Spakfilla, we often have to cross a wall of what linguists call 'phatic speech'. They define this as any expression that performs 'a social task' rather than one that conveys real information. Which is just the sort of weak-kneed explanation that linguists come up with for a useless piece of Manglish.

The 'social task', most of the time, is to break the ice – to establish the relationship between two speakers by exchanging words that neither of them means in any literal sense. We ask 'How are you?' even when we are not interested in a reply, and we answer 'Good' even when our best friend just died in a car crash and we've been diagnosed with a stage-five melanoma. Then we comment on the weather. According to linguists, it is only by going through these opening exchanges that we can bond sufficiently to get on with the business of communicating actual content. Here are some common phatic forms:

How's it going?

How've you been?

Looks like it might rain.

I'm getting sick of this heat.

Not content with our home-grown Spakfilla, we are also starting to import it from overseas, and we apply it thickly at several stages of a conversation. We blame globalisation. Corporations have discovered they can fill an entire customer-service transaction with expressions they never really mean:

Do you mind if I put you on hold?

Have a nice day.

How may I be of service?

We value your feedback.

Your call is important to us.

The Quakers may have been onto something when they argued for plain speech that goes straight to a practical purpose: 'Let your words be few' was their maxim. So next time you decide to comment on the weather or inquire about someone's health, consider whether you can perform this ritual opening with words that actually mean something.

PRONOUNCEEASHUN

How utterly bizarre is it that 'pronunciation' is one of the most mispronounced words in the English language? And why do so many of us confuse the verbs 'to buy' and 'to bring' when they become 'bought' and 'brought'? Why could George W. Bush never pronounce 'nuclear', and (more importantly) why did half of his senior staff start pronouncing it 'nucular'? Probably for the same reason that some Spaniards speak with a Castilian lisp. Or was that an urban myth about a Spanish king who spoke with one?

We will always be arguing about the way that words should be pronounced. We should keep doing so. While most people who say 'aitch' are very aware of those who say 'haitch', the latter appear to be quite unaware of the former. Originally an Anglican-versus-Catholic obsession, even the *Macquarie Dictionary* now accepts 'haitch'.

But there remain many examples of mispronunciation that continue to create uncertainty about the intended meaning. While recognising that this is one of the ways in which languages evolve, there are plenty of words worth preserving just as they are. Espeshully if we are to keep our pronounceeashun even remoterly connected wiv our spelling:

Abattor
Abattoir

Ackshally
Actually

Admittably
Admittedly

Advocado
Avocado

Alaminimum
Aluminium

Albun
Album

Amatcher
Amateur

Ameniable
Amenable

Ampitheatre
Amphitheatre

Anenome
Anemone

Anethetist
Anaesthetist

Angerling
Angling

Antartic
Antarctic

Anythink
Anything

Archetypical
Archetypal

Ardamant
Adamant

Artic
Arctic

Artitect
Architect

AMPITHEATRE

Arx/Arst/Arxed
Ask/Asked/Asked

Ascetic
Aesthetic

Asselerate
Accelerate

Assembaly
Assembly

Assept
Accept

Assessory
Accessory

Astericks
Asterisk

Atherlete
Athlete

Austraya/Straya
Australia

Authorative
Authoritative

Balloowuns
Balloons

Bassic
Basic

Beholding
Beholden

Boatique
Boutique

Briyant
Brilliant

Bronichal
Bronchial

Brureaucracy
Bureaucracy

Burgular
Burglar

ANGERLING

Cans
Cairns

Capsicun
Capsicum

Carcogenic
Carcinogenic

Celry
Celery

Cerebal
Cerebral

Certainy
Certainly

Characterture
Caricature

Chooseday
Tuesday

Clapse
Collapse

Close/Cloves
Clothes

Collary
Colliery

Congradjulations
Congratulations

Conshume
Consume

Contempry
Contemporary

Contractural
Contractual

Cruzants/Cruzonts
Croissants

Cumberbun
Cummerbund

Curve
Kerb

Cutelry
Cutlery

Daybyou
Debut

Definately
Definitely

Deteriate
Deteriorate

Dewarf
Dwarf

Dias
Dais

Diptheria
Diphtheria

Dipthong
Diphthong

Drawring
Drawing

Drownding
Drowning

Entrepeneur/ Entreprenure
Entrepreneur

Erogeneous
Erogenous

Escavation
Excavation

Esculate
Escalate

Esculator
Escalator

Estatic
Ecstatic

Everythink
Everything

Exclusitivity
Exclusivity

Exerts
Excerpts

Exetra/Essetera
Et cetera

Expresso
Espresso

Exscape
Escape

Extraterrestial
Extraterrestrial

Eyetalian
Italian

Fabalous
Fabulous

Fambly
Family

Febuary
February

Filum
Film

Fission
Fishing

Fracksher
Fracture

Fufill
Fulfill

Gamberling
Gambling

Geneology
Genealogy

Govament
Government

Grievious
Grievous

Growen
Grown

Height-th
Height

Hostible
Hospital

Humbrage
Umbrage

Hundret
Hundred

Hyderangea
Hydrangea

Icelated
Isolated

Igzillary
Auxiliary

Ingine
Engine

Intergestion
Indigestion

Intermediatries
Intermediaries

Intraveneously
Intravenously

Itinery/Itinry
Itinerary

Janry
January

Jest
Just

Jewel
Duel

Knowen
Known

Lenth
Length

Letcher
Lecture

Libry/Libery
Library

Mandareen
Mandarin

Manerfacture
Manufacture

Maximun
Maximum

Medium strip
Median strip

Menestration
Menstruation

Mingerling
Mingling

Minimun
Minimum

Mischievious
Mischievous

Miwyon/Miwlyon
Million

Munce
Months

Nasturtians
Nasturtiums

LETCHERER

Nectareen
Nectarine

Nelegible
Negligible

Nelly
Nearly

Nothink/Nuffink
Nothing

Nucular
Nuclear

Obstroperous/ Obstropulos
Obstreperous

Ony
Only

Opporchunity
Opportunity

Ow
Our

Owers
Hours

Pantomine
Pantomime

Paps/Praps/Prehaps
Perhaps

Particuly
Particularly

Pasgetti
Spaghetti

Pavalova
Pavlova

Penist
Pianist

Pentathalon
Pentathlon

Perculator
Percolator

Perf
Perth

Perogative
Prerogative

Pervent
Prevent

Phenomenum
Phenomenon

Pickernick
Picnic

Pitcher
Picture

Pleese force
Police force

Prade
Parade

Predeliction
Predilection

Preshume
Presume

Proberly/Probly
Probably

Pronounciation
Pronunciation

Pry minister
Prime minister

Punkin
Pumpkin

Pursoo
Pursue

Ramsack
Ransack

Reconise
Recognise

Refrectory
Refectory

Reguly
Regularly

Relevation
Revelation

Reservor
Reservoir

Respitry
Respiratory

Restrong
Restaurant

REFRECTORY

Revebrations
Reverberations

Rhododendrum
Rhododendron

Riseling
Riesling

Rooly
Really

Samwich
Sandwich

Sawring
Sawing

Scrip
Script

Script
Scrip

Secketry/Seckertary
Secretary

Self-opiniated
Self-opinionated

Semellon
Semillon

Seri Lanka
Sri Lanka

Sewerage
Sewage

Sex
Sects

Showen
Shown

Simily
Similarly

Stastistic
Statistic

Stomick
Stomach

Strenth
Strength

Subsidary
Subsidiary

Surface Paradise
Surfers Paradise

Suspose
Suppose

Suspused/Esposed
Supposed

Sussinct
Succinct

Synney/Sydeney
Sydney

Tempeture
Temperature

Temprally
Temporarily

Tempry
Temporary

Torturous
Tortuous

Triffic
Terrific

Typerwriter
Typewriter

Umberella
Umbrella

Unequivocably
Unequivocally

Unrule
Unreal

Veecle
Vehicle

Vetinary
Veterinary

Vinegarette
Vinaigrette

Vunerable
Vulnerable

Watercrest
Watercress

Westminister
Westminster

Woite woine
White wine

X-eray
X-ray

Yuge
Huge

Yuman
Human

Yumorous
Humorous

Zackly/Eggzackly
Exactly

MALAPROPS AND GENERAL MANGLISH

While most mispronunciations bear some resemblance to the original word, sometimes Manglish leads to a completely different meaning. The worst of these are malaprops.

Malaprops

Malapropisms are best defined by their originator, Mrs Malaprop, in Richard Brinsley Sheridan's play *The Rivals*. Accused of decking 'her dull chat with hard words which she don't understand,' she replies: 'Sure, if I reprehend anything in this world, it is the use of my oracular tongue, and a nice derangement of epitaphs.'

Some of these are very common and have been occurring for decades. Others are relatively recent, and a few are one-off coinages by people grappling with the language. Malaprops mangle the most when they create an entirely new and unintended meaning:

Accept
Except

Airzone layer
Ozone layer

All intensive purposes
All intents and purposes

Antidotes
Anecdotes

Antipasta
Antipasto

Anti-semantic
Anti-Semitic

Aquapuncture
Acupuncture

Artheritis
Arthritis

Ashfelt
Asphalt

Batter/butter an eyelid
Bat an eyelid

Brassiere
Brasserie

Buttered to death
Battered to death

Candelstine
Clandestine

Casting nasturtiums
Casting aspersions

Catermeringue
Catamaran

Chaise lounge
Chaise longue

Choirpractor
Chiropractor

Chomping at the bit
Champing at the bit

Cup of chino
Cappuccino

Depository
Suppository

BUTTERED TO DEATH

Diabeets
Diabetes

Double ammonia
Double pneumonia

Dry-reaching
Dry-retching

Ediface complex
Edifice complex

Erroneous zones
Erogenous zones

Fowl swoop
Fell swoop

High dungeon
High dudgeon

Ice-cream comb
Ice-cream cone

Imminent
Eminent or prominent

Insinuendo
Innuendo or insinuation

Judicial
Judicious

Macandamien nuts
Macadamia nuts

Mahogamous
Monogamous

Minuet lettuce
Mignonette lettuce

Muted
Mooted

Mute point
Moot point

Obnoxious weed
Noxious weed

Off her own back
Off her own bat

Old timers' disease
Alzheimer's disease

Orgasm
Organism

Pacifically
Specifically

Plutonic
Platonic

Proprietary
Propriety

Proscribe
Ascribe

Prostrate
Prostate

Quaterzone
Cortisone

Reality
Realty

Reconnaissance
Recognisance

Renumeration
Remuneration

Revelant
Relevant

Sheath of flowers
Sheaf of flowers

Shock exorber
Shock absorber

Slithers of beef
Slivers of beef

Succeed
Secede

Sucking pig
Suckling pig

Tenderhooks
Tenterhooks

Title wave
Tidal wave

Transcendental medication
Transcendental meditation

Unindated
Inundated

Vagrancies of the situation
Vagaries of the situation

Water on a duck's back
Water off a duck's back

Woe to go
Go to whoa

General Manglish

The philosopher Jeremy Butterfield once said: 'Grammar is often a generic way of referring to any aspect of English that people object to.' Some would argue that he meant to say 'any aspect of English to which people object'. British politician Sir Winston Churchill would disagree. When receiving a corrected memorandum drawing attention to a sentence ending with a preposition, Churchill responded: 'This is offensive impertinence, up with which I will not put.'

There is an important distinction between grammar and usage. Some of the shibboleths of old-school grammar turned out to be simplistic rules that we taught to keep our kids under tight control during the rise of compulsory education. It's in fact quite feasible to have a preposition at the end of a sentence, as Churchill argued. And even Shakespeare started a fair proportion of his sentences with conjunctions. It's just that most of the time it's better not to do these things.

Some complain about how the American term 'gotten' is rapidly invading our lexicon. But why not? Shakespeare used it. And we're quite happy to use 'forgotten' and 'ill-gotten'.

Nevertheless, as with all Manglish, fundamental rules of grammar will always remain, and these are much harder to justify breaking. They include maintaining parts of speech that we shouldn't confuse, verb forms worth keeping just as they are, prepositions that needn't change, and word usage that is already perfectly clear. Watch out for these forms of grammatical Manglish:

Better had
Had better

Bet to
Better

Better of
Better have

Continually
Continuously

Continuously
Continually

Could of
Could have

Either do I
Neither do I

Here's two
Here are two

He's own
His own

Hone in
Home in

I never
I did not

Irregardless
Regardless

I rung/I've rang
I rang/I've rung

Laying down
Lying down

Lend
Loan

Loan
Lend

Me own
My

Of a night
At night

Or right
All right

Should of
Should've

So fun
Fun

So not
Not

There's two
There are two

A whole nother
Another

Would of
Would've

Yeah-no
Yes or no

Youse/youses
You

SPORTSPEAK

You have to feel some sympathy for sportsmen and sportswomen. They train hard. They get injured. They break through pain barriers, and they collapse in despair when they lose a game or a race. Then, just as they are desperately sucking in oxygen, some bloke in a leery lime-green jacket thrusts a microphone in their face and asks: 'What happened out there today?'

What else can a team player do but fall back on the standard post-match clichés?

> Yeah, well, we knew we had to dig deep and give it 110 per cent, but we made too many errors and didn't stick to our game plan. So from here on we have to keep focused and regroup because it's do or die. We've really got our backs up against the wall and we're in a must-win situation. But we have to treat it like any other game and can't worry about other results.

But sympathy for the sportsperson puffing through a post-match interview quickly dissipates when you get to the press conference. That's when you realise that the clichés are likely to be the smartest things they say.

Players

Grown men who chase balls – footballers in particular – are in a league of their own when it comes to mangling the language.

Sometimes it's not the team's average IQ that is 100, it's the aggregate. How else can we explain this sort of analysis?

Defensively, I think it's important for us to tackle.

Ninety per cent of the game is half mental.

Some should definitely leave medical questions to the team doctor:

I've never had major knee surgery on any other part of my body.

Therapy is a good thing. It can be therapeutic.

And definitely avoid talking about the team:

Me and George and Billy are two of a kind.

Some guys are inwardly outgoing.

Or about themselves:

I'm the most loyal player money can buy.

I may be dumb, but I'm not stupid.

No-one but an athlete can truly understand the nature of winning:

Winning doesn't really matter as long as you win.

Or, for that matter, losing:

I would not be bothered if we lost every game as long as we won the league.

We must have had 99 per cent of the match. It was the other three per cent that cost us.

The gold and silver medals for humility must surely go to these sportspeople:

I really lack the words to compliment myself today.

I'll always be number one to myself.

Yet it's the personal insights that we appreciate the most:

I had to overcome a lot of diversity.

I want all the kids to copulate me.

I owe a lot to my parents, especially my mother and father.

And if it all goes wrong, you simply blame the media:

Sometimes they write what I say and not what I mean.

That picture was taken out of context.

I don't care what the tape says. I didn't say it.

Until:

One day I'll get someone to write my autobiography.

SOMEONE WRITING MY AUTOBIOGRAPHY

Coaches

Success in sport often comes down to the tactics of the coach. There are the coaches who can explain their failures:

> Better teams win more often than the teams that are not so good.

> We are on the crest of a slump.

For them, next season will always be better:

> We're going to turn this team around 360 degrees.

> You can sum up this sport in two words: you never know.

They are candid about their failings:

> I made a wrong mistake.

> Most of my clichés aren't original.

> It isn't like I came down from Mount Sinai with the tabloids.

Yet they always understand their team so well:

> He's a guy who gets up at six o'clock in the morning regardless of what time it is.

He's about the size of a lot of guys that size.

And they always keep the team in line:

You guys pair up in groups of three, then line up in a circle.

I'm the coach around here and don't you remember it.

While they stay on the right side of the game:

We're not trying to circumcise rules.

I'm not allowed to comment on lousy officiating.

At their best, they rival even the greatest philosophers:

You've got to be very careful if you don't know where you're going, because you might not get there.

Commentators

In the great league of sportspeak, it's the commentators who take out the gold medal. This is understandable, given that they do most of the talking, and have the handicap of having to describe essentially the same actions over and over and over.

How can you describe another close contest? Simply select from the official list of commentator clichés:

Anything can happen on the day.

It's a game of cat and mouse.

It's a game of inches.

It's a nailbiter.

It's a shame somebody has to lose.

It's crunch time.

The real winner today was [insert sport here].

They're fighting tooth and nail.

They're going at it hammer and tongs.

They're within striking distance now.

This could be the turning point.

This is where experience will come to the fore.

This one is going down to the wire.

Those desperate to come up with some fresh words are at even greater risk. Under the pressure of a live broadcast, they will inevitably come out with some of the dumbest things, starting with comments about the weather:

The wind was completely still.

It's only a light shower, or a downpour, really.

They work themselves up to talking about the crowd:

It's a partial sellout.

The crowd's been let in free today and they're certainly getting their money's worth.

Next comes an attempt to set the scene:

The racecourse is as level as a billiard ball.

This is an interesting circuit, because it has inclines. And not just up, but down as well.

Then, analysis of the players and athletes:

She forces her opponents to make unforced errors.

He's amphibious in the field — he throws with both hands.

His two biggest strengths are his legs, his speed, his agility, and his competitiveness.

They are always searching for the exact word. Or at least a shortlist:

He ran straight through the open gap with nobody in it.

He seems to have suffered a groin injury at the top of his leg.

I'm amazed that he was the only one singled out.

The referee's trying to separate them apart.

The triple, yes, that's three consecutive tackles in succession.

You've been a crowd-pleaser to a lot of people.

The action itself cannot escape the numerical precision of the commentator:

Her time is about 4.33, which she's capable of.

Ninety percent of putts that are short don't go in.

The lead is now 6.9 seconds. In fact, it's just under 7 seconds.

Then there are sentences that should never have been formed in anyone's head:

Ah, isn't that nice, the wife of the Cambridge president is kissing the cox of the Oxford crew.

That is a really lovely horse. I once rode her mother.

This is Gregoriava from Bulgaria … I saw her snatch this morning and it was amazing.

Few sports can rival rugby in New Zealand:

He's looking for some meaningful penetration into the backline.

There's nothing that a tight forward likes more than a loosie right up his backside.

You don't like to see hookers going down on players like that.

Finally, the post-match wrap takes it to the next level:

Any time they score 100 points and hold the other team below 100 points, they almost always win.

A lot is said about defence, but at the end of the game the team with the most points wins, the other team loses.

Nobody in football should be called a genius. A genius is a guy like Norman Einstein.

Sure, there have been injuries and deaths in boxing, but none of them serious.

To which we can only conclude:

You might not think that's cricket, and it's not. It's motor racing.

FOODSPIEL

Friends are coming over for dinner, so you trot down to the supermarket to buy the ingredients for Nanna's good old deep-dish pie. You wander over to the pastry section, but the words 'ambient sausage roll' on a packet catch your eye. Exactly how does an ambient sausage roll differ from a normal one? Does it make you feel relaxed and comfortable? Perhaps it was baked in a kitchen featuring New Age music, tantric chanting, and sandalwood incense?

It turns out that 'ambient' just refers to a food that can be stored at room temperature. The label might mean a lot to people stacking shelves, but not much to anyone else. Except perhaps to those who wonder what might be in a sausage roll that can be kept at room temperature.

Food language uses plain words, but it becomes Manglish when it confuses the very consumers it is supposed to help. A survey recently found that 80 per cent of us rely on the labels on packaging as our main source of information about food. Yet only 40 per cent of us understand food labels, and a third of us can't tell the difference between an advertisement and genuine nutritional information. Which explains your problems in shopping for the deep-dish pie.

Confusing Consumer Labels

Undaunted, you move on to the meat section, but are immediately confused by two labels:

Best before

Use by

Who would have thought that 'use by' means that a product is unsafe to consume after expiry, yet 'best before' foods are still safe to eat after the listed date?

So you decide to make a fish pie, only to encounter more confusion with the seafood labels:

Made in Australia

Product of Australia

Would you believe that only 50 per cent of a product actually needs to be produced and manufactured in the country for it to carry the 'Made in Australia' label? Yet all 'significant' ingredients and processing must be Australian if it is a 'Product of Australia'.

Your confusion turns a shade of green in the aisle where the flour is kept, when you encounter words like 'biodynamic', 'ecological', and 'organic'.

These words don't seem all that mangled, but their meaning certainly is. There are more than eight 'organic' certification schemes in Australia, and none uses a consistent definition.

But that's nothing compared to the complexity you face when you get to the eggs:

Barn-laid Cage-free Eggs

Bio-organic Free-range Eggs

Cage-free Liberty Eggs

Environmental Eggs, Caged

Farm Eggs Natural Living Free Range

Field Fresh Certified Free-range Eggs

Free-range Eco Eggs

This apparently has something to do with a chicken's ability to express herself while she is environmentally caged or biodynamically ranging. Before we eat her eggs.

Labelese

And what about dessert? You decide on fruit salad and coffee with fresh cream. But there's no escaping the Manglish of foodspeak here, as you encounter the following labels:

Made with fruit ingredients

Real coffee, ice-cold

'Made with' and 'real' imply that the featured ingredient is a significant part of the product. In fact, these labels often highlight a minor element.

Then there is '93% fat free'. A 'low-fat' product should contain less than 3 per cent fat. At 93 per cent, a product is neither low in fat nor particularly healthy. Funnily enough, we never read '7% fat' on a packet.

There is also 'lite' and 'light'. 'Lite' does not usually mean lower in fat or energy, but rather signals something about the texture, colour, or taste of a product. This is commonly applied to oils, to imply they are lower in fat when they aren't. Unfortunately, that 'lite' olive oil is still 100 per cent fat.

Then there's 'less sugar' and 'reduced fat'. 'Less' doesn't actually mean 'low'. It just means at least 25 per cent less than the original, which can still be quite a lot. For example, your cake might have 25 per cent less sugar than a cake with 90 per cent sugar, but that's still a lot of sugar.

You console yourself that your dessert has 'full coffee taste' and 'real fruit flavour'. Yet the words 'taste' and 'flavour' hide a multitude of ingredients. They usually shout 'real fruit' or 'full coffee' in large type, only to add the qualifers 'taste' and 'flavour' in miniscule text printed in a hard-to-see combination such as yellow on white. The fruit and coffee content may be negligible.

Dinner at home is looking less and less attractive. Maybe you should all eat out.

Menuspiel

Unfortunately, the Manglish of foodspeak continues as soon as you sit down to read the restaurant menu. A 'menu engineer' has finetuned this menu so that you will spend as much as possible. They started with the colour: apparently red and blue stimulate the appetite, while grey and purple stimulate feelings of contentment. So there's lots of red by the main dishes, and a muted purple next to the desserts.

Then there is the trick of placing the most expensive dishes at the top of the menu, or in a prominent box. Sometimes they are accompanied by images. So when your eye is drawn to that colourful chilli icon, you've just been had.

Then, you start reading the menu descriptions and strike the carefully crafted 'enhancers':

Applewood-smoked bacon pie with home-style farm fresh eggs
Bacon and egg pie

Beer-and-honey-battered dusky flathead, baby rocket, sauce gribiche, and lemon wedges
Fish of the day

Apparently, four descriptions get us salivating more than anything else:

Someone's name
Mama Puchinni's homemade Tuscan ciabatta

A geographic label
Freshly shucked Pambula rock oysters

A sensory label
Liquid-butternut gnocchi with sage and mushroom consommé

A nostalgia label

Home-style slow-roasted chicken and oven-baked vegetables

Restaurants have also learned that we are likely to spend more when there are no dollar signs next to each dish's price. We'll have that entree for 24 but not for $24. Of course, in the poshest of the posh places, the prices are not listed at all.

Suddenly, even an ambient sausage roll seems a more appetising prospect.

SILLY SIGNS

In the world of publishing, it is axiomatic that the larger a piece of text, the more likely that it will contain an embarrassing error. Forget everything you imagined about proofreaders failing to spot an errant footnote in two-point type. It's the 200-point mistakes that they are going to miss.

Nowhere is this better illustrated than in signage. We see them everywhere, every day. They are generally large. Yet somehow, signs with the most egregious errors manage to get through the whole process of typesetting, production, and installation without anyone noticing. Then everyone gets the chance to notice.

Stating-the-bleeding-obvious Signs

The first type of silly sign comes from the school of thought that we wouldn't know if the sun is shining without a sign. There was this helpful road sign:

CAUTION: WATER ON ROAD DURING RAIN

And this, at a bar:

NOTICE — PUBLIC BAR
Our public bar is presently not open because it is closed.
Manager.

Then, on a door:

IF DOOR DOES NOT OPEN DO NOT ENTER.

Signs That Over-elaborate Appliances

At the other end of the spectrum are the signs that go on and on about how impressive their host appliance is. These are particularly prevalent in public toilets, such as this notice on a hand dryer:

> How it works — we have achieved the best possible performance by using the available power supply and holding the air velocity to a level which will allow it to heat to the highest temperature near [what] dry hands could stand on a warm day. This produces the driest air, giving the maximum rate of evaporation.
>
> Why it varies — because of the initial temperature and humidity of the air, and the amount of moisture on your hands.

It's unlikely we would be able to use a tap without this:

This fixture may deliver hot water which will scald.

Or know what to do here without a comprehensive tract:

Flick Washroom Services

This system is maintained by using the latest in sanitising treatment methods.

This affirms that you, the user, can at all times have the peace of mind that a high standard of hygiene is being met.

To help us better maintain this facility for your use and that of others.

Please flush after use.

And heaters certainly need detailed explanation:

SAFETY NOTICE
This heater will get hot.
Please take note and for your own safety do not touch the unit.

Stupid Warning Labels

While we're on the subject of warnings, have you noticed the Manglish that often appears in the guise of product labels? Some can't help but state the obvious:

Open packet. Eat contents. (on a packet of peanuts)

In order to get out of car, open door, get out, lock doors, and then close doors. (in a car manual)

The appliance is switched on by setting the on/off switch to the 'on' position. (on a kettle)

Others really make you wonder what people get up to on a rainy day:

May be harmful if swallowed. (on a shipment of hammers)

Warning: do not attempt to swallow. (on a mattress)

Do not use while sleeping. (on a hair dryer)

Or whether manufacturers have actually faced lawsuits for the following:

Do not attempt to stop the blade with your hand. (on a chainsaw)

Do not use this product during an earthquake. (on a disposable razor)

Caution: do not use near powerlines. (on a toilet plunger)

And did anyone seriously think about the following labels?

Remove infant before folding for storage. (on a stroller)

Not to be used for the other use. (on a food processor)

Do not turn upside down. (on the bottom of a product)

Self-contradictory Signs

Of course, warning labels are hardly alone in making little sense. One retailer couldn't make its mind up:

STORE CLOSING
NOW HIRING

There's a reason quarriers don't go to university:

BOTTOMLESS PIT
65 FEET DEEP

Defence personnel would be uncertain at a military base:

Restricted to unauthorised personnel

Shoppers looking for parking would be confused by:

ENTRANCE ONLY
DO NOT ENTER

Only to confront this when they reach the shops:

Customers should use push buttons to open automatic doors.

Illiterute Protest Sings

The latest trend in silly signs involves the intellectual endeavours of a grass-roots political movement in the United States. They are supremely confident about their point of view, if not their spelling and grammar:

Respect Are Country
Speak English

We wonder what the Moran family did that was so offensive:

Get a Brain!
MORANS!

And whether they might ever forgive Hugh:

One Hugh Mistake America

It seems that the Wers are particularly upset:

Wer Not Going to Take it

Probably because:

We're Loosing our Constitutional Rights

And demanding:

No Pubic Option
No Amnety

And petitioning Congress to:

Shred Your Taxing Scholiast Policies

We can only conclude that if you want to influence people in power, at least learn how to spell what you object to.

Signs That Nobody Thought Through Properly

Finally we come the five-star, logic-defying signs, notices so silly that you wonder what the writers could possibly have been thinking. There was this roadside billboard:

ILLITERATE?
WRITE FOR FREE HELP
ILLITERACY FOUNDATION

And a useful sign in a hospital:

FAMILY PLANNING ADVICE
USE REAR ENTRANCE

A local pharmacy proudly boasted:

We dispense with accuracy

When a local newspaper drew attention to the unintended meaning, the wounded pharmacy huffily changed its sign to:

We don't dispense with accuracy

And at a golf course for postmodernist logicians:

DO NOT LEAN GOLF CLUBS AGAINST SIGN

MANGLISH CHRISTMAS CAROLS

Every December, the soul within every mangler gets a gentle tug in the direction of clarity. So they huddle together festively by forming workplace choirs. They hire halls to rehearse in. Eventually, they put on faded Santa hats and cluster in the foyers of skyscrapers to share their songs.

This process starts well enough, with song sheets taken from traditional carols. But somewhere during rehearsal, it is felt that 'it would not be inappropriate in relation to the purposes of communication' to update the lyrics in a manner that better reflects the expertise of the modern professional.

So each chorister is allotted a carol to rewrite in 21st-century argot, being fully cognisant of the requirements of the contemporary bureaucrat, scientist, academic, auditor, business analyst, and lawyer.

Here are their carols.

From the Bureaucrat

Memorandum

It would be appreciated if all persons pertaining to belief and not insignificant states of gladfulness would, in the fullness of time, proceed by appropriate means to the location of

Bethlehem in observance of the personage whose natal event coincided with his recommended appointment as the supreme monarch of angels. It would be further appreciated if persons proceeding to the said location would be in triplicate adorement pursuant to his sovereign status as Christus Deus.

Translation

O come all ye faithful, joyful, and triumphant
O come ye, O come ye, to Bethlehem.
Come and behold Him, born the King of Angels;

O come let us adore Him
O come let us adore Him
O come let us adore Him
Christ the Lord.

From the Scientist

Contained within a feeding receptacle for ruminant domesticated animals without the full benefit of a bassinet to be recumbent upon

The diminutive Christus Deus endeavoured to repose his
nacreous cranium.
The supernovas commenced emitting lambent light in the
luminous heavens and regarded the location of recumbrance
Whilst the diminutive Christus Deus was insensible within a
faggot of vegetation of the genus *Graminae*.

Translation

Away in a manger, no crib for a bed
The little lord Jesus laid down his sweet head.
The stars in the bright sky looked down where he lay
The little lord Jesus asleep in the hay.

From the Poststructuralist Academic

The semiotic coding of the other can be reflected in the
assignation of binary opposites in the chronological nocturn
Which can be characterised as either quiescent and voiceless,
or multisonous and stentorian
However, these can be resolved into the former only where
the nocturn exhibits the sanctified, imperturbable, and
refulgent cultural plane wherein the desexualised m/other
and her sanctified, self-controlled child
May attain the meaning of unified, almost sidereal, aestivation.

Translation

Silent night, holy night
All is calm, all is bright
Round yon virgin mother and child
Holy infant so tender and mild
Sleep in heavenly peace.
Sleep in heavenly peace.

From the Auditor

It would be preferable if it is observed but not lamented
If the lips are not thrust with sullenness because of the following reason
In the near future, the diminutive metropolis will be visited by a rotund, vermilion-clad gentleman.

An enumeration is being made, the contents of which will be confirmed on two occasions
It will be ascertained which persons of limited chronological advancement have been non-compliant and which have been compliant
In the near future, the diminutive metropolis will be visited by a rotund, vermilion-clad gentleman.

It is observed when persons are being insensible
It is known when persons are being insomnious
It is ascertained when persons are compliant and non-compliant
So it is recommended that consideration be given to the pursuit of compliance.

Translation

You'd better watch out, you'd better not cry
You'd better not pout, I'm telling you why
Santa Claus is coming to town.

He's making a list, he's checking it twice
He's going to find out who's naughty and nice
Santa Claus is coming to town.

He sees you when you're sleeping
He knows when you're awake
He knows when you've been bad or good
So be good for goodness sake.

From the Business Analyst

The content will be delivered by a multifaceted program combining novel paradigm outcomes powered by the 'rhinoglow' engine. Platform users and developers applied disempowering nomenclature to the earlier version of rhinoglow.

However, the Christmas release of version 2.1 will, according to the chief operating officer, facilitate a clearer delivery mode and content guidance in relation to B2B requirements, which will impact user scenarios in terms of unparalleled benchmarks.

Translation

Rudolph, the red-nosed reindeer, had a very shiny nose
And if you ever saw it, you would even say it glows
All of the other reindeer used to laugh and call him names
They never let poor Rudolph join in any reindeer games.

Then one foggy Christmas Eve, Santa came to say
Rudolph, with your nose so bright, won't you guide my sleigh tonight?
Then all the reindeers loved him, and they shouted out with glee
Rudolph, the red-nosed reindeer, you'll go down in history.

From the Lawyer

We are desirous of extending to you by way of seasonal salutation, in respect of which we undertake to convey by means including but not limited to speech, writing, hand signals, electronic devices, and any other information conveyances in existence now and in the future, a sanguine and unrepining saturnalian season and a euphoric neologian period of not less than but not more than twelve (12) months, including such adjustment as from time to time may be necessitated by leap years where appropriate.

Translation

We wish you a merry Christmas
We wish you a merry Christmas
We wish you a merry Christmas
And a happy New Year.

As do we all at *Modern Manglish*. And may the rest of the year be mangle-free.

ACKNOWLEDGEMENTS

There's something almost therapeutic about collecting mangles. Since our language is subject to the daily assaults of gobbledygook, the simple act of recording each example seems a small but satisfying step towards clarity. More importantly, it brings us into contact with others who share the love of our language.

For helping to find, expose, or clarify modern Manglish in all its forms, we would like to thank the following people alphabetically: Richard Ackland, Geoff Bolton, David Brunches, Robbie Buck, Kate Burridge, Sue Butler, Peter Butt, Alex Buzo, Steven Caires, Patrick Cook, Robert Eagleson, Richard Fidler, Kate Foord, Ross Garnaut, Bryan Garner, Michelle Grattan, Matt Haig, Lynda Harris, James Lambert, Richard Lederer, Michael Lewis, Bill Lutz, Angela Michaelis, Daniel Oppenheimer, Patricia Robertson, Peta Spear, John Stewart, Hedley Thomas, Ken Thomson, Diane Wallis, Annie Warburton, David Wessel, Harry Williamson, and Richard Woolcott. Special thanks also go to Simon Blackall, who edited the original *Manglish*, and to Clarence Brown for research on much of the new material.

For being regular sources of Manglish, we would like to thank newspapers such as *The Sydney Morning Herald*, *The Age*, the *Herald Sun*, the *Australian Financial Review*, *The Courier-Mail*, *The Australian*, *The New York Times*, *The Guardian*, and *The Times*. Of the broadcast media, we give particular thanks to the ABC local radio network, and ABC television news and current affairs. Thanks also go to websites such as buzzwhack.com, engrish.com, jobs2view.com, missionstatements.com, and urbandictionary.com.

We'd also like to thank the staff of our respective organisations, the Plain English Foundation and the Pedestrian Council, for putting up with the writing of this book during a busy year.

And of course, where would we be without acknowledging the primary source for this work: the manglers themselves. We have seldom named the individuals we quote throughout the book to protect the less-than-innocent. If some of the words we've highlighted sound close to home, remember that you are not alone and that recognition is the first step to better public language.